**REVISED EDITION**

# AFRICA
## It's True Role in the Ancient World

### An Informal Analysis

By:
Matthew Theodore Momon

Africa: It's True Role in the Ancient World
Copyright © 2024 by Matthew Theodore Momon

All rights reserved. No part of this publication may be reproduced, distributed, or transmitted in any form or by any means, including photocopying, recording, or other electronic or mechanical methods, without the prior written permission of the author, except in the case of brief quotations embodied in critical reviews and certain other non-commercial uses permitted by copyright law.

ISBN
978-1-964393-11-7 (Paperback)
978-1-964393-12-4 (eBook)
978-1-964393-16-2 (Hardcover)

# AFRICA
It's True Role in the
Ancient World

# TABLE OF CONTENTS

Preface ..................................................................................... vii
Introduction ............................................................................... xi

| | | |
|---|---|---|
| Section 1 | Intervention .................................................................. 1 | |
| Section 2 | Discovery ....................................................................... 9 | |
| Section 3 | Ice Age: The Evidence ................................................ 17 | |
| Section 4 | The Pyramid Complex ................................................ 27 | |
| Section 5 | Attack of the Persians ................................................ 41 | |
| Section 6 | The Truth about Alexander the Great ...................... 47 | |
| Section 7 | An African Mystery System: Electrical Engineering ....... 59 | |
| Section 8 | The Past ...................................................................... 65 | |
| Section 9 | Carthage: Kingdom of the Moors ............................. 75 | |
| Section 10 | Rome, the Conjecture ............................................. 85 | |
| Section 11 | My Thoughts ........................................................... 101 | |
| Section 12 | The Arab Invasion .................................................. 107 | |
| Section 13 | European Saviors: Granada, Salamanca, Timbuktu and the Rosetta Stone. The Significance of the Zodiac ......................... 115 | |
| Section 14 | 165 Philosophers and 50 Artisans ........................ 143 | |
| Section 15 | The Black and White I.Q. ....................................... 147 | |
| Section 16 | The Nemi Ships ...................................................... 151 | |
| Section 17 | European Contribution to Society ....................... 163 | |
| Section 18 | Today and Beyond ................................................. 167 | |

About The Author ................................................................... 179
Special Thanks ........................................................................ 181

This book is the truth as I have come to know it over the years.

# PREFACE

To begin, let me state that I do not allege expertise of being either a writer or historian. I am just observant to the complexities of life, social conditions and issues, global perceptions of cultures, as well as credited and discredited contributions of African people. It is the mathematics and science training I received that has made me question the historical perspective promoted by Europeans or mainstream media regarding Africa's true legacy.

Fortunately, what I have observed over the last thirty years, from 1976 to 2006, are aspects of history that have been made available to everyone. Unfortunately, many of the African people are just too busy to pay attention or even care about these historical corrections but once the African people have been made aware of these new facts it will change accepted perceptions of themselves. I have observed important reexaminations of a previously accepted version of the past in documentaries from "In Search of" to "The History Channel" and in several books about Africa and the African's contributions that have also provided a wealth of overlooked data that I highly recommend. Refer to the 'Special Thanks' page of this informal book for enlightening and informative reading. These resources have helped me see past the European perspective to the truth of Africa's past. I also have obtained fifty hours of DVD documented evidence from these television channels and other assets as a resource.

Additionally, I have detected distortions and discontinuities in Africa's timeline, once I recognized that time is continuous. I also became cognizant of the deliberate attempt to separate Egypt from its continental homeland of Africa. Some people would have you believe that the country of Egypt was not part of the physical body of Africa's continent. Yet, the island of Britain (England and Scotland) and the island of Ireland are both a part of the continent of Europe and not attached to the physical body of Europe. This is extremely puzzling. Moreover, Europe is the only continent that does not fit the definition of a continent (one of the principal landmasses of the earth). Europe does however fit the definition of a peninsula (a long projection of land into water connected by a narrow strip of land). Therefore, why is Europe called a continent?

Furthermore, the only source that the common man can find stories about this region surrounding the Mediterranean Sea is the Bible, and it is written in allegorical form. Allegorical form is a form in which people, things and events have a symbolic meaning that can be molded any way the writer wants. This is truly a means of distorting the truth in the favor of others with a hidden agenda. In short, I have detected gaping holes in our world's religious and academic systems concerning their origins in this part of the world and no one has claimed responsibility for creating this accepted confusion or declared that there is any confusion in the first place to be clarified. For me, one question surfaces: how is it that Africa and Europe are so close to each other and yet have no common history? Hence, there has to be much more to this than meets the eye. So, my hunt was on for the solidification of Africa's true past.

However, even after coming into contact with new information, I was still not prepared to preserve or record it. Yet, one day in the winter of 2005, I was sitting down relaxing when suddenly 20,000 years of the past hit me in the face in two quick seconds. I cried uncontrollably. It was then that I decided to write down what I learned in summation format. After discussing my proposal with others, and desiring to present my information to students, I was asked by Dr. Timothy Caruthers to lecture on part of Africa's legacy to his philosophy class at Wayne County Community College District in Detroit, Michigan. Although I was reluctant, I gathered myself and spoke to the class. With encouragement, I now continue my quest to enlighten others.

People will say that my book is based on speculation and unfounded evidence and therefore should not be seen as scholarly or factual. I say history (his-story) has been written by those who have hanged heroes. I say the Europeans version is a hoax trumped up to make him look superior, to make up for his inferiorities. Did you know that this version of lies is considered scholarly and factual by the academic community and has been accepted as truth for over 2,000 years?

Moreover, the European is the academic community controlling what is learned. In truth, I have learned that Europe is really the dark territory making little to no positive contribution to mankind. It is everything the African continent has been called over the years, over the centuries. It is time to decide for yourself what the truth really is.

# INTRODUCTION

This book is designed to assist the advanced mathematics and science students through the maze of the Ancient World/Hellenistic World/Classical World and its flow into the Modern World. This book will not only put critical events in perspective but also in their true chronological order. This book will give the reader knowledge of the history of the Mediterranean World from the Persian Empire to the 1883 A.D. discovery of electricity and beyond. From the seven wonders of the ancient world to ancient warfare and ancient machines of war and peace to Africa's development and implementation of the disciplines of mathematics, all engineering sciences, physics, chemistry, metallurgy, statistics, medicine, masonry, technology, ethics, political science, metaphysics, astronomy, astrology and philosophy.

In general, the reader will be introduced to a world that was developed and maintained by the mind of the African. This way of thought has maintained the world up to the modern age. Most importantly, the reader will learn through deductive and inductive reasoning where the origin of the western world really begins—who educated whom, when this education took place, where it took place, how long this educational environment lasted, the manner in which the professors and master teachers were treated, when the course of the world changed, who changed it, how it was changed and why. If the reader is tired of "**Keep your eyes on the Prize!**" and wants to know what the prize is and whether or not the African deserves the prize, then read this book and be informed.

For your edification, all Bible verses come from the NKJV.

Africa: It's True Role in the Ancient World an Informal Analysis by Matthew Theodore Momon is an intelligent and thought provoking book. This book will create lots of discussion. The best way to enjoy this book is to have a bible along with pencil and paper to conduct the mathematical calculations. The book is written with great passion and enthusiasm. The author should teach a class regarding that subject to share his passion and knowledge.

Respectfully considered and submitted,
Dr. Carol Dabner.

This book was first published and copy written in 2012 A.D.

# SECTION 1

# Intervention

Since I have been teaching math and science as a tutor, teacher and a professor, I have learned that people have a fear or phobia for these subjects, particularly so for mathematics. The college students that desire to become mathematicians, scientists and students of fields related to mathematics, all want help in understanding its essence. These students should know that the math they have to digest is universal. Most students want to know the tricks they've missed somewhere in their educational careers that will allow them to see the subject's secrets clearly so they can apply it in the real world or pass it on to their students.

I have traced the root of this math phobia to childhood and I have realized that if the elementary school students learned to like mathematics as they do Spanish, French and Chinese then they would accept math at more than just face value. They would see math as a vehicle to a better life instead of a barrier in front of it. The people who have direct access to these children are the elementary school teachers. If these teachers do not like mathematics then this kind of philosophy or phobia will spread to the student and the cycle will repeat.

To prevent this heinous crime from happening, again, the elementary school teacher must be targeted. Since they have to be college students also, they need to know the inner workings of this subject. This subject has the potential to frighten individuals throughout their lives if no intervention is performed. These individuals need to know the properties of mathematics, what kind of numbers these properties work on, how to use these properties on those numbers and the real result in real world situations. These real-world situations include, but are not limited to, engineering, physics, statistics and probability theory, chemistry, stochastic processes, linear and non-linear algebra, queuing theory, inventory theory, duality theory, simplex method, reliability and decision analysis.

The college students do not want to be treated like children. In my experience, after the students have seen the inner workings of math and understand it, they have a feeling of pride and self-confidence in the subject and most want to know more. Then they want to try it on their own. By the end of their collegiate math careers, they are confident, fearless, self-reliant and self-assured critical thinkers about the subject of math. They also feel ready to pass their experiences to the next generation either in application or in education. This understanding of mathematics has not been experienced by the average African for 2,100 years and needs to be addressed. The potential of the math process for Africans either in America or elsewhere is immeasurable. So, I've decided to turn this process inward on itself to find its **kinetic**.

It is clear to me the African's freedom and education world-wide has been controlled from without. The African is not encouraged to know his basic rights given to him by the Bill of Rights and the Constitution of the United States of America and neither of his mental contribution to the development of these documents or even his contribution to the very development of the Office of the President. He is not taught to be independent or to think independently. He is taught that he is inferior and believes it because there is seemingly no proof of the contrary. By claiming not to have the resources to improve inner city schools and the areas around them, children do not feel safe and at the same time have a comfortable living and learning environment to study in. Instead, the European would rather build state of the art stadiums, casinos and prisons. Psychologically, this is depressing—to be made to feel unwanted and useless to mainstream society, these

*Africa: It's True Role in the Ancient World*

messages are heard loud and clear by most Africans, especially the educated ones.

The exclusion of the African contribution starts for most people with American history. Most people do not know that there are over 2,000 patents earned by Africans between the years 1865 A.D. and 1940 A.D. running the alphabet from A to W. Yet, this does not include the patents that Africans should have received during slavery. Instead, Africans were called a credit to their race at that time. Needless to say, the African inventors did not receive patents because Thomas Jefferson said they were considered property and worth only three-fifths of a man or sixty percent. Thanks to Thomas Jefferson and his alteration of the Declaration of Independence, the African had to also wait another 89 years for his freedom. Nevertheless, the people that received credit for those inventions were the slave owners. Even today, the African is not taught his own accomplishments. In his own mind he is only worth fifty percent of a man or half a dollar.

Here are a few accomplishments made by African inventors. Africans like John Hanson (First President of the United States of America) appointed George Washington as Commanding General in the Revolutionary War. He also made Thanksgiving a holiday, designed the Great Seal which is on the one-dollar bill and every document signed by the Office of the President to conclude laws decided on by the Supreme Court. He invented the concept of democracy together with the office of the presidency and all conditions laws and authority under the title. He is also on the two-dollar bill. Benjamin Banneker, a freemason, inducted George Washington into the Freemasonry Lodge in Virginia 1752 A.D. George Washington appointed him to design and plan out the District of Columbia and the Capital Building, carved a wooden clock with all wooden gears that kept perfect time for fifty years. No wonder the clock tower in London England is named after him. He also wrote two bestselling books titled "Banneker's Almanac" that both out sold Benjamin Franklin's almanacs.

Elijah McCoy invented the automatic lubrication for steam engines, coined the phrase "It's the real McCoy". Jan Matzeliger created the first machine for mass-producing shoes. Granville Woods holds 35 patents for electromechanical devices, bringing about improvements in telegraphs, telephones, automatic cutoffs for electrical circuits and electric motor regulators. Alexander Mils invented the elevator. Richard Spikes created the automatic gearshift for cars and Joseph Gambol invented the super charger system for internal combustion engines.

Albert R. Robinson invented the electric trolley, the procurer of the rapid transit system. Charles Brooks made the street sweeper, John Love, made the pencil sharpener, William Purveys, made the fountain pen and hand stamp. Lee Barrage made the typewriting machine, W.A. Love, the advanced printing press, Philip Downing, the letter drop. Joseph Smith invented the lawn sprinkler and John Burr made the lawn mower. Frederick Jones came up with the modern-day air conditioner, Alice Parker, the modern-day furnace, Michael Harvey, the lantern, Thomas

W. Steward, the mop, Lloyd P. Ray, the dust pan, Walter Sammons, the comb, Sarah Boone, the ironing board. George T. Samon invented the clothes dryer, John Standard made the refrigerator, Lewis Latimer created an inexpensive cotton thread filament, which made electrical light practical for homes and businesses.

Garret Morgan created the first automatic spotlight and a smoke inhaler mask. Lewis Temple, moveable harpoon-head which revolutionized the whaling industry, Fredrick McKinley Jones, moveable refrigerator unit that transformed the food transport industry, Otis Boykin, the control unit in artificial heart stimulators and an electrical device used in all guided missiles and IBM computers, Meredith Gourdine, a pioneer in energy conversion, inventor of many products and processes based on the use of electro-gas-dynamics technology. Dr. Mark Dean is in the National Hall of Inventors, Vice President with IBM, architect of the modern personal computer, holding three of the original nine patents on the computer that all PC's are based upon making the PC practical for homes and small businesses. Recently, he made history again by leading the design team responsible for creating the first one-gigahertz processing chip.

Let us not forget about the geneticist, the multi-genius George Washington Carver who patented three hundred products from the peanut and another 150 products from the sweet potato and changed agricultural practices all over the world. Not to mention his discovery of soy as a renewable fuel for automobiles that could also be used to replace the materials for the exterior, interior and tires.

In 1997 A.D., 75 years after, Henry Ford begged George Washington Carver to be a part of his developmental team. The Ford Motor Company then developed a soy-powered car that was almost made entirely of soy except for the engine, the chassis and the power train. This cars' top speed was a racy 150 miles per hour.

As you can see even in this short list, African Americans have made significant contributions to science despite the absence of at least two basic conditions for scientific work; #1 Freedom from full-time pressures for personal survival and #2 A stimulating cultural environment. Unfortunately, these great modern-day African inventors, despite their accomplishments, are going through history anonymously as if they did not exist and had nothing positive to contribute to society.

If the African ever has questions about himself, he has to do his own research—the research that should be mandatory in public schools, especially in the inner cities. This needs to be done so that the African can look beyond the 140 years of mis-education and misinformation, the 423 years of slavery in America, the 100 years of slavery by the Arab, the 500 years of slavery in Rome, the 265 years of slavery in Egypt by the Hyksos (white people from Northern Israel), the constant disturbances by the Hittites (white people from North of the black land of Canaan). Both happening between the 12$^{th}$ and 17$^{th}$ dynasties, where they were both later exiled by the Pharaohs Ahmose I and Ramesses II respectively and the last 1,900 years of religious persecution so that the African can discover that he/ she is the most harmonic, intelligent and important person to walk the planet. Indeed, that if the African American were to go back to Africa and take his/her patents with them, America would collapse under its own weight. For this reason, the African has been put into a box of educational constraints in order to control him and to stop him from reaching his full potential. I think a very good question is where did this natural intelligence of the Negro slave come from anyway and is there any evidence of it ever revealing itself before the African was ever oppressed?

*Africa: It's True Role in the Ancient World* •

John Hanson, American Patriot and First President of the United States (1715-1783)

John Hanson

This is the false portrait of John Hanson. Now you can see how far the Europeans will go to cover the truth. The only saving grace here is when you look him up on a Google search, you can read about the man that was John Hanson.

Here is a portrait of the real John Hanson. It is a daguerreotype, a process used to take pictures before film. Look him up at www.loc.gov then search John Hanson daguerreotype and you will see him too.

Portrait of the Signing of the Declaration of Independence

Notice how European John Hanson is in this portrait of the signing of the Declaration of Independence. He is the one seated in the middle of the first row with a tan suit on behind the only desk with documents hanging from it. He has a feather pen in his hand, a bottle of ink, and documents spread out on his desk. Why is his ethnicity an issue?

> According to the Washetaw Tribe, the Presidents of the Continental Congress that lived between John Hanson and George Washington include Elias Bondinot, Thomas Miffin, Richard Henry Lee, John Handcock, Nathaniel Gorham, Arthur St. Clair, and Syrus Griffin were all Moors. I just can't find the pictures to prove it.

# SECTION 2

# Discovery

All throughout history, the African has been told that the African continent has made little or no contribution to civilization. He has been told he is the germ carrier, the personification of a criminal, and as a human being he is inferior and of the lowest order. This is done to control the thinking of the African because as a man thinks, so he is. The African is made to see himself as nothing in general, save perhaps an athlete, musician, actor or singer. So, in general, he will be nothing and therefore not a threat to the European order.

Some other questions in every educated African's mind should be why? Why has the European done all these horrible things to the African? How long has the European been doing this to the African? Why do Africans live so poorly today? Is it because the Europeans know more about the Africans past than the Africans?

Only now after 2,100 years is the truth coming to the surface. Let's start with the First Trinity in human history which is the trinity that all Popes pray to in private, the legendary holy royal family of Africa, which consists of Horus, Ausar, and Aset. This family of black people is best known by their Greek names Heru, Osiris, and Isis. There are many versions of this story but there is one based on mathematics and science. It has been written that at the time of Osiris' birth, a voice was heard throughout the land proclaiming that the lord of creation was born. He is recognized as a great king of Africa who brought civilization to his people and established a code of laws and instructions for the worship of God. He ruled Africa, the land of the blacks, along with his wife Isis for 450 years.

According to legend, Osiris was slain by his cunning and evil brother Set (Seth), who cut his body into fourteen pieces. He then tossed his phallus and scrotum into the Nile River where they were later consumed by a catfish, then scattered the rest of his body parts throughout Africa to prevent him from having an heir to the throne. For some reason, it wasn't enough to just kill Osiris. Isis barely escaped with her life. After finding out what happened to her husband, Isis gathered together a team of scientists to find the most important part of her husband's body, that part that included the duct work where the sperm is stored for excretion. She knew she only had three days to extract the sperm or it would be too late.

The royal scientists found that particular body part, extracted the sperm from the ducts and an egg from Isis, mated the proper sperm with the egg to create a male child, and then inserted the zygote into Isis. This operation was symbolized by the obelisk, which later became a symbol representing the resurrection of Osiris. This is because the Obelisk is in the shape of the device used to hold her open during the operation. Meanwhile, Set (Seth) and his army took over the kingship of Africa, making life miserable for all of its inhabitancy.

Isis was without child before the murder of Osiris, before the operation. Nine months later Isis gave birth to a son that she named Horus (Heru), who after years of preparation in hiding, gathered together an army and avenged the death of his father by slaying his evil uncle Set (Seth) and reestablishing his fathers' kingdom. In an act of divine inspiration, Heru did not put Sets' army to death for treason. Instead he exiled them from the land of Africa into the frozen wastelands beyond the Mediterranean Sea. Heru's deeds were so inspiring, so well-known by the European elite, the freemasons, that when it came time to declare a basic unit for the American money system the American elite, and the freemasons decided to put Heru's name, the name of the world's first hero, the name that the word hero comes from, on the back of the dollar bill in hieroglyphs as a joke on the African, the ones who do not remember who they are now.

During the American Revolutionary War in 1776 A.D., there were 14 black freemasons. These black freemasons were equal to or better than the white ones. They also aided in the development of the American rights and policies that we hold so dear today. If I were you, I would find out who the white ones were, then you will know that during these depressive and oppressive times the level the black ones had to attain. Back in the time of Heru, the people of Africa were so happy to be freed by Heru, after 350 years of oppression under Set's rule, they fashioned the largest freestanding statue in the world and put his head on it. We know this statue today by its new name, the Sphinx. Then Heru ruled Africa for 300 years.

This statue was made to represent man's ability to suppress his beastly, animal instincts in order to reach a higher level of consciousness, to enable him to see the world without time. The body of a lion was chosen because the lion is the king of beasts. The Africans topped it with the head and face of a man, the face of the world's first hero, Heru, the son of Osiris, slayer of the evil one and restorer of order from chaos.

This statue known as the Sphinx, is 265 feet long and 65 feet high and has been estimated by the new age Egyptologists to be 19,500 years old. They say that the Sphinx is an earthly representation of the constellation Leo. The Sphinx enclosure represents the horizon, which separates or blocks off that part of the Sphinx that can't be seen in the constellation Leo when the sun rises. In other words, the constellation Leo is an early morning constellation, some degrees south of east and rises to a point on the horizon but never fully rises because its image is blocked out by the intensity of the morning sun. The Sphinx is facing almost due east and is supposed to see his own image in the early morning sky. According to the American Heritage Dictionary of the English Language, the word horizon is from the Greek Horizō and is the present participle of Horizein, to divide or separate from horos. It has been calculated that the Sphinx could see its own image dead on, eye to eye, in the early morning sky starting in the year 17500 B.C.

Today, the constellation Leo has moved further south from its previous position of eye contact with the Sphinx due to the last polar shift. This phenomenon will be explained in detail in the next section.

The new age Egyptologists do not believe the old date of 3000 B.C. that mainstream Egyptologists say is the starting point of African history for a host of reasons. Mainstream Egyptologists also say in the same breath that the Pyramid Complex was constructed around 2750 B.C.

This means that the knowledge of where and how to design and build these structures was developed and mastered in only 250 years. Before this time period, Africans were nomads clubbing their women in the head and dragging them into caves. This discrepancy regarding the age of the Pyramid Complex and their roles as tombs for the Pharaohs is the largest of lies and has been accepted as truth for too long. Today, they have raised the number of years to design and complete these structures from 250 to 1,000 to compensate for the new knowledge base about the Pyramid Complex that is continuously seeping out to the world like a dripping water faucet.

Based on my research on the African and my unique knowledge of mathematics, physical science, biology, operations research, probability theory and statistics, I will tell you the truth as I know it to be and where this same evidence will take you if you allow it to.

When Set was slain by Heru, Set's army was exiled to the frozen wastelands beyond the Mediterranean Sea in 17500 B.C. This date is recorded by the very presence of the Sphinx and its relationship with the constellation Leo. Most laymen have heard of the Ice Age and some even know that climatologists say that it ended around 9500 B.C. This would mean that Set's army was in that wasteland for at least 8,000 years. They lived 8,000 years in cold temperatures, cloudy skies and living at least 1.5 miles above sea level by virtue of the very glacier that covered Europe and the Caucus Mountains at that time. Exposed to these conditions for that length of time, Set's army would no longer need their dark skin to protect them from the sun's radiation. They also would no longer have a need for thick noses to breathe cold dry air, nor would they need their thick lips to cool the air as it passed into the respiratory system. They would become what they are generally today—pale skinned, thin nosed, thin-lipped people.

It is unlikely for a person to become tops in the fields of Anthropology, Archeology or Egyptology and not come to this conclusion based on the evidence. It should be noted that the European Paleontologists and Paleo zoologists claim to know the migration, mating, and dietary habits of many dinosaurs as well as their appearance and yet these scientists have never seen any in action on the grounds that these mega beasts have been extinct for 65,000,000 years. So, are we to assume the Europeans know nothing about the epoch of humanity, the origin of himself as well as the origin and way of life of the great black man before him? I wonder...

The Majestic Sphinx as it peers into the sky at its own image, the Constellation Leo

Note: The Great Pyramid of Giza is in the background

*Africa: It's True Role in the Ancient World* •

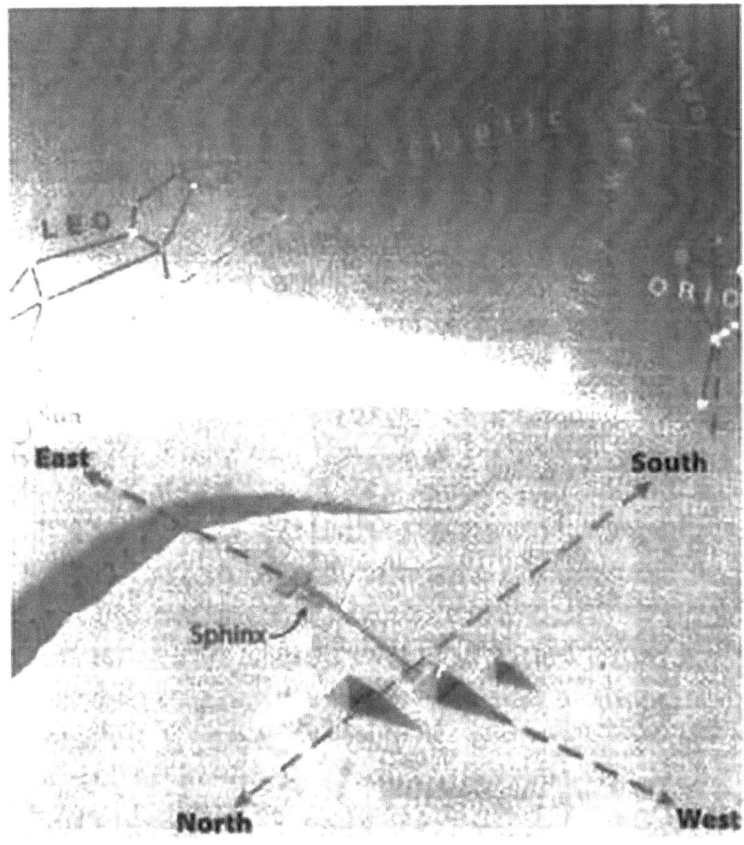

The primary monuments on Egypt's Giza plateau map the celestial configuration of the vernal equinox sunrise (March 21) of 10500 B.C. This map positions the vernal equinox sunrise in Leo and places Orion on the true prime meridian of the earth at sunrise. On the earthly plane, the Sphinx is Leo, the Nile River is the Milky Way Galaxy (Our Galaxy?) and the three Giza Pyramids are the belt of Orion. Note that the Sphinx is on the wrong side of the river Nile. This is proof that the Sphinx is much older than the pyramids and their purpose. The magnificent Egyptians combined these two time periods flawlessly on the vernal equinox of 10500 B.C.

• *Matthew Theodore Momon*

African Names:   Horus     Ausar     Aset
Greek Names:     Heru      Osiris    Isis

# SECTION 3

# Ice Age: The Evidence

Climatologists say that the Ice Age ended around 11,500 years ago but they neglect to say how. ***Scientists and Egyptologists*** also say that Egypt was not old enough to have experience the Ice Age. There is a theory in climatology, however, that explains the end of the Ice Age, the lack of eye-to-eye contact between the Sphinx and the constellation Leo and the real reason for the construction of the Pyramid Complex.

This theory is based on the discovery of plate tectonics. Plate tectonics is the regular movements of the earth's major landmasses caused by the earth's rock cycle. Volcanic eruptions, earthquakes, fault lines and rifts are caused by this rock cycle phenomenon. The theory says that there were times in the past when the systems of plates move as one unit or all together due to an uneven mass distribution i.e. the mass of the glacier that made Hudson Bay and the Great Lakes. Scientists call this event Crustal Displacement or simply the Polar Shift. This event is not unrealistic because there is only thirty miles of rock separating the surface of the earth from its mantle or liquid rock.

The Gulf Stream is a river that flows in the North Atlantic Ocean, north of the equator. It is 50 miles wide 2 miles deep at its maximum with a maximum flow of 5.6 miles per hour. This is faster than the speed limit of Eight-Mile road in Detroit, Michigan during rush-hour. This flow of water does a myriad of things. The obvious is it sends the warm waters of the equator pole ward and warms the European sub-continental atmosphere. The Gulf Stream is powerful enough to be readily seen from space.

Now, salt in water, on the other hand, does not create a surface heat flow. Salt in water creates a depth heat flow and the Atlantic Ocean is 3 miles deep on average. So, salt has little to do with the flow of this river phenomenon. But that's not the point. The point is that if this surface flow of the Gulf Stream ceases then Europe's weather system will become cold again, as it was during the Ice Age. Europe is the key to this uneven mass distribution because it is clearly not bound by the original Arctic Circle and yet it was completely covered by ice about 2.5 miles thick at that time (see pg 20).

The hurricanes that come to America every year come from the heat of the Sahara Desert flowing over the tropical Atlantic Ocean into the Gulf Stream. The heat picks up water vapor and humidity that is pushed up into the atmosphere due to the heat of the ocean that is heated by the Sun. It begins to spin counterclockwise caused by the spin of the earth, like our toilets if you live in the Northern hemisphere. This disturbance then follows the Gulf Stream across the Northern Atlantic picking up speed, energy and size. The Gulf Stream is forced northward by the continental shelf of North America. The shelf is effectively a wall in its way. However, the flow of the atmosphere is generally not affected by this wall, yet the hurricanes generally flow from south to the north anyway. These hurricanes are pushed back to the Atlantic Ocean by the Canadian Jet Stream every year. So, the Gulf Stream even affects the American weather systems every year primarily in the fall.

The Ice Age happened. The evidence exists in the appearance of the Great Lakes, Hudson Bay, and the Canadian boulder debris left at the Tennessee/Kentucky border and in New York's Central Park. These boulders are only prevalent 2,244 miles north of their current position. These anomalies make it feasible to interpret a straight-line distance perpendicular to the Tennessee/Kentucky border, the distance of the diameter of the Arctic Circle. This straight-line distance is approximately equal to the distance from a point in Central Alaska all the way to the northern tip of Sweden. If this straight-line distance is drawn on the real globe of earth, in the direction of 90 degrees north from the Tennessee/Kentucky border, with the center of this perpendicular line found, one can then rotate this line on its center. A new Arctic Circle has just been made with its center at 60N latitude, 80W longitude, right in the middle of the Hudson Bay. Observe the area that the new Artic Circle takes up. The northern flow of the Gulf Stream is bound by this circle now, this circle of ice. This will stop the flow of the Gulf Stream, sending Europe back into its frozen tomb. The question is what will this do to Africa?

It was the shifting of the earth's surface that melted the ice sheet in the Atlantic Ocean that started the flow of the Gulf Stream in the first place. The Gulf Stream is the phenomenon that sends warm weather into Europe's sub-continental atmosphere. This warm, wet weather is prevented from entering into Africa by the Atlas Mountain Range. Amazingly, this mountain range, which has a maximum height of 13,665 feet, and a maximum length of 1,553.4 miles not only separates the Sahara Desert from the Mediterranean Sea but also the weather systems coming from the northwest i.e. caused by the Gulf Stream.

This is one of the reasons that the Sahara is a desert today. These mountains act as a tri-fold barrier; they also allow the trade winds that blow from east to west to race unimpeded across the face of North Africa into the Atlantic Ocean. These winds race swiftly between the equator and 25N latitude completely drying out the region. This desert is the largest desert on earth today, covering an area of 3,500,000 square miles and if it were 200,000 square miles larger, it would be equal in area to Europe. Before this shift, the Sahara received this weather making the Sahara a tropical savanna (i.e. Eden as described in the Bible.) I wonder what kinds of kingdoms were lost in this region because of this phenomenon. Nevertheless, the Sahara has been a desert for only 8,000 years as confirmed by sonar and radar mapping.

After reading Genesis (2:10-15) know this, the river Nile is the River Pishon and Gihon. Also, Havilah is a son of Kush (Genesis10:7) Kush is a son of Ham (Genesis 10:6) and Kush is Ethiopia. Furthermore, Ethiopia is a word from the Greek meaning sun burned faces. And in the Ancient World, Ethiopia was all of the region known as the Sahara and the region known as Mesopotamia according to the Greeks, where, the other two rivers, Tigris and Euphrates, flow through. Mesopotamia simply means the land between the Tigris and Euphrates Rivers. This is where the Lord put man. I must point out that the Atlantic Ocean, on the west side of Africa and the Indian Ocean, on the east, were both known as the Ethiopian Sea before the 1500's A.D.

Moreover, Kush begot Nimrod who ruled over Shinar (Genesis 10:8-10). Shinar is in Sumeria and Sumeria is Mesopotamia. European scholars say that Nimrod is related to the Pharaoh Semerkhet of the 1st Dynasty. African scholars say that Nimrod is the Pharaoh Semerkhet who set up a kingdom in Mesopotamia. His people were known by the prefix of his name; Sumerian or Semerian. The previously mentioned are all of the land of Eden.

If we think critically about this now, a line drawn from the center of the new Arctic Circle perpendicular to that new Arctic Circle will drop through the earth and will exit at 60S latitude, 80E longitude in the southern Indian Ocean. Draw another line equal to the diameter of the first line of rotation then rotate it on its center. Now witness the new Antarctic Circle after this is completed. If you are paying attention, a new continent will emerge from the depths of the unseen now in the latitudes that receive sunlight. These new Arctic and Antarctic circles are actually the original Arctic and Antarctic circles before the last polar shift.

Remember the spin of the earth's core is constant, negating a slight wobble. The earth's core is a magnet with north and south poles called Magnetic North and Magnetic South. This is where the Northern and Southern lights are. These poles are not the same as Geographic North and Geographic South. Geographic North and South are made up by man to encompass those regions on the earth's surface that are the coldest. Mathematics and Science have already proven that the Nile that flows from Lake Victoria on Mount Kilimanjaro, north to the Mediterranean Sea used to flow west from Lake Victoria on Mount Kilimanjaro to the Atlantic Ocean as the red line depicts on the cover of this book. There is a huge ancient river gorge that can be seen with sonar and radar left over from its wake.

This means that the spin of the earth and its core were unaffected by the geographic polar shift. This implies everything. This is the main reason why the Sahara is a desert today. The only way this westward flow of the Nile was possible is if the earth's surface had a different orientation with respect to its magnetic poles than it does today. After performing this procedure on a globe, the best orientation for the observer to see the truth, if you still can't see it, is to stand on your hands. While upside down now, and not disturbing the globe, you will see Africa as it is configured on the cover of this book. You will also see the hidden continent, the one you've heard about but questioned or ignored all your life, reappear in the southern latitudes that receive sunlight. Today it is known as Antarctica, now under 2.5 miles of ice effectively under water. This continent is the famous Atlantis that disappeared from the earth's surface around 11000 B.C. so says the ancient Egyptian Hieroglyphs, as this language spoke of the other black continent that vanished from the face of the earth. The reason why you should stand on your hands is because the Africans declared south to be the top of the earth, not the bottom as it is today. The European tried to hide these facts by destroying most of the writings of the University of Alexandria's professor of history, Mer-enjuiti, and then they literally flipped the earth upside down so that Europe would be on top of Africa and soon after, they developed the Mercator Projection Map to make Europe appear bigger than a now shriveled up *Africa.* They did this to appear superior to the African.

Thank God the Africans were thorough people and wrote these facts about Atlantis on the walls in stone for the ages. It is why we even entertain the notion of this lost continent in the first place. This lost continent was said to possess the highest technologies known to man: everything we have today and more. Edgar Casey, a modern-day prophet who passed away in 1945 A.D., tells us that Atlantis even had a renewable power source that stored sunlight for future use.

This is not farfetched at all. We know of five renewable energy sources we could use right now. They are Solar, Wind, Wave, Tidal and Geothermal. Any one of these energy sources could power the earth indefinitely. The only reason we are unaware of their true potential and therefore not using them is because of big oil and the other corporations of the world including the bank. They cannot profit from these unlimited extremely abundant power sources, so these institutions, to maintain their bottom line, down play their potential. Nonetheless, the Europeans are still looking for the kingdom of Atlantis.

The Original Arctic Circle (Before the last polar shift)

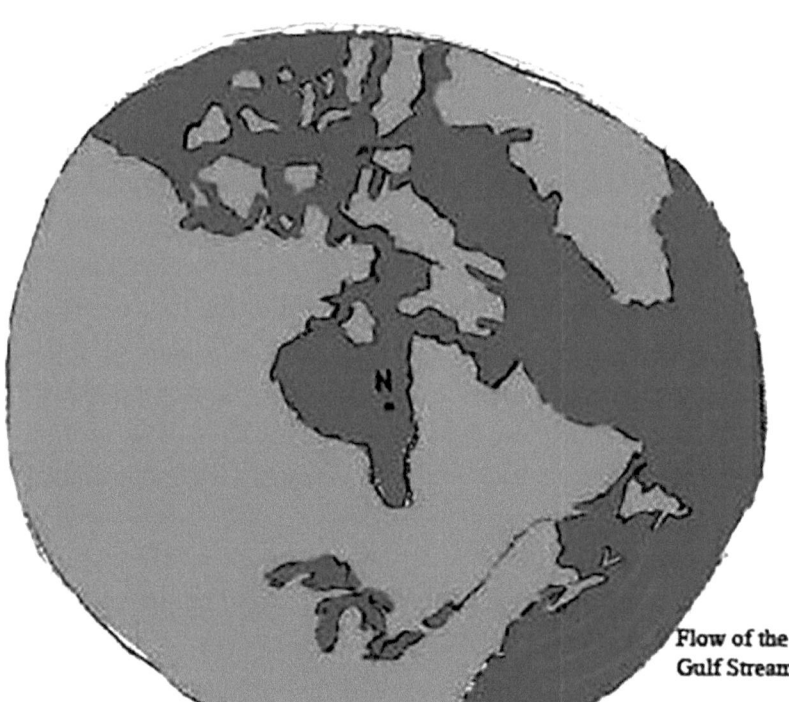

Flow of the Gulf Stream

Based on what the European has said since 1976, since I've started paying attention, I have calculated that the original position of the North Pole was 60N latitude 80W longitude, directly in the middle of Hudson Bay, Canada, with the Arctic Circle clearly illustrated. This is when the Sahara Desert was a tropical savanna. The Sahara Savanna was a fact for countless eons before the last polar shift 13 to 14,000 years ago. The question is what other kingdoms in Africa were lost when the Sahara Savanna became the Sahara Desert?

It is interesting to note that there are pyramids and ancient megalithic structures all over the world except North America. Why? The Europeans did not destroy them because if he could, he would have destroyed them all. North America was a frozen wasteland.

*Africa: It's True Role in the Ancient World* •

The Original Antarctic Circle (Before the last polar shift)

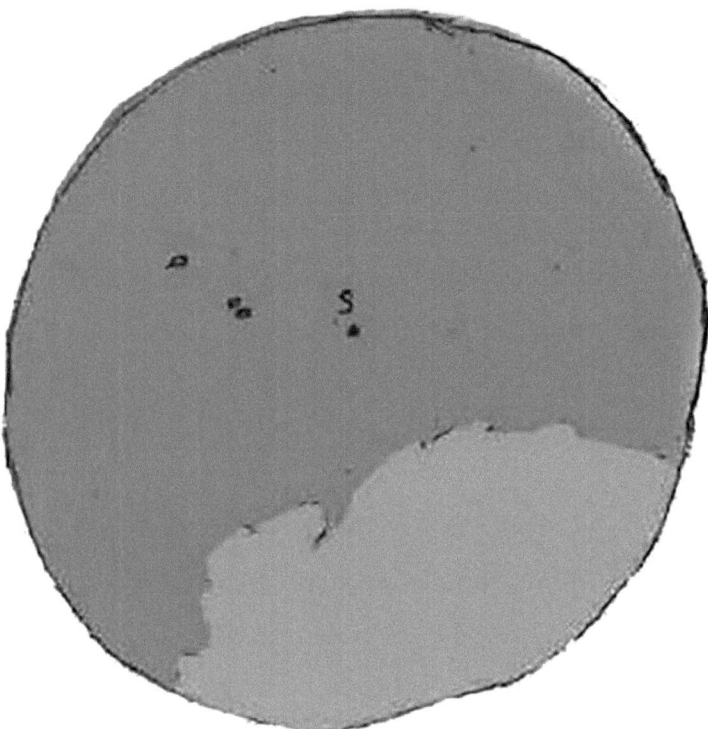

Based on what the European has said since 1976, since I've started paying attention, I have calculated that the original position of the South Pole was 60S latitude 80E longitude, directly in the middle of the Southern Indian Ocean, with the Antarctic Circle clearly illustrated. If attention is paid to this image, one can see that Antarctica is no longer bound by the Antarctic Circle. This is when and where the Kingdom of Atlantis saw sunlight for countless eons before the last polar shift 13 to 14,000 years ago.

This is my educated guess at the flat map of the world before the last polar shift. It was not easy by any means but for a better picture, I would have to have a custom globe made to my specifications so I could then cut it open along its lines of longitude and then lay it flat. One day I will.

*Africa: It's True Role in the Ancient World* •

The Piri Reis Map

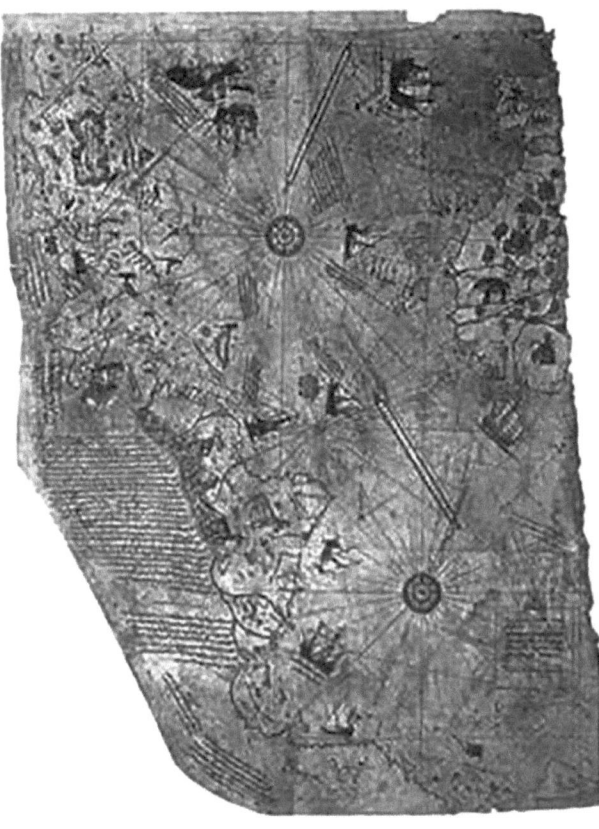

The Piri Reis Map, shown above, is the oldest surviving map to show the Americas. It is not European, surprisingly, but Turkish. It bears a date of 919 in the Muslim calendar, corresponding to 1513 A.D. in the Western Calendar. It is in the Topkapi Palace in Istanbul, formally Constantinople. The map was stolen from the Library of Alexandria from a larger collection of world maps of which only Colonel Piri Reis Map remains. The map was lost for a long time and only rediscovered in the 20th century. Apart from its great historic interest, the map has been alleged to contain details no European could have known in the 1500's and therefore proves the existence of ancient technological civilizations.

## The Piri Reis Map, an Abstract View

Scholars say the Piri Reis map is accurate to within a 1/2 a degree of longitude at the equator. Well, if there are 60 minutes in 1 degree of longitude at the equator and 1/2 minute is 3,043.8 feet, according to the Great Pyramid of Giza. It follows that a minute must be 6,087.6 feet. This implies that 30 minutes (1/2 of a degree of longitude at the equator) is 182,628 feet or 34.6 miles. The rate at which Africa and South America are moving away from each other is known to be 1 inch per year. This means that the age of the source maps that Piri Reis used to make his map had to be at least 2,191,536 years old. You may find this calculation to be outrageous but may I remind you that the European used the same technique to determine when Africa and South America were one landmass i.e. 225 million years ago. How did he come up with this number? Simple, all he needed was the rate of separation and the present distance between the two continents in inches. Note that this map differs from modern maps of the Atlantic Ocean. The Piri Reis map shows more islands and a different geological North and South America. Why? The answer: The water levels were much lower when the original maps were drawn.

# SECTION 4

# The Pyramid Complex

And God, which has set signs and wonders in the land of Egypt even onto this day Jeremiah (32:17-20). Around 12000 B.C. the earth's crust shifted about 2,244 miles to the south due to the mass of the glacier which extended from the present-day North Pole to the southern border of Kentucky. This diameter would then be rotated to create a new arctic circle. In some places, the ice was estimated to be three miles thick. Since the ice was on land, i.e. North America and Europe, water levels in some places around the world were estimated to be 500 feet lower than they are today. This shift is also responsible for all the flood stories all over the world including Noah's, Genesis chapters 6, 7 and 8, subsequently creating the current world map.

This shift is what made the present-day world map. But, by depicting the continent of Africa with a tilt as it was before the shift it would satisfy two conditions; it puts the Sphinx in perfect alignment with the constellation Leo as it was intended by the designers to mark its place in time as well as justify the ancient flow of the Nile River in its northern path to the present-day Atlantic Ocean. This description is illustrated on the cover of this book. This shifting of the earth's crust compelled the people of the world to design and build an indestructible, immovable object that could withstand any earthquake.

This object could remain a reference point to mark the position of the earth's crust after the last polar shift, to mark the position of the earth with respect to itself, the sun and stars. This would be a footprint of the people of earth to remind future generations that it is possible to make earth into heaven. It's what you make of your situation that is important and the African made the situations and the conditions of the people more important than the individual. We must work together to survive; we are an organism. This is a hive mentality and it is the complete opposite of the thinking of today.

The Great Pyramid of Giza is that marker. Its footprint is on the true prime meridian of earth. The prime meridian separates all the landmasses equally, a line of longitude that becomes the dateline when it falls through the Bering Strait and into the Pacific Ocean on the other side of the earth. It rests at the center of the longest **land** meridian (0 degrees longitude which is again, the true prime meridian of earth) and the longest **land** parallel on the globe (30 degrees N latitude), dividing the earth's land masses into equal quarters in terms of area. Incredible. The Great Pyramid also lies at the center of gravity of all the continents. Meaning, if you cut the globe open, and laid it flat, like a map, with Africa at the center, one could balance the map on their finger underneath it. The Great Pyramid is the most perfectly aligned building to true north than any building ever designed. The alignment is only 1/12 of a degree off true north, which is about 5.76 miles off, if you were to walk from the north face of the Great Pyramid north to the North Pole. This misalignment has been attributed to the regular movement of the African continent since the Great Pyramid's construction and not an error on the part of those who constructed it. That means that after the Great Pyramid was constructed, one could walk headlong into the geographic North Pole from its north face. It is also a perfect pyramid with a perfect square base and perfect isosceles triangular facets.

The Paris Observatory is the most perfectly aligned structure built in modern times and it is aligned six minutes or 1/10th of a degree off true north about 6.93 miles. This means that if you walked to the North Pole from the north face of the Paris Observatory you would miss the North Pole by 6.93 miles. How is it possible that "slaves" or primitive workers accomplished a feat, thousands of years ago, where "skilled" technicians would have difficulty doing today? It is because the Great Pyramid is a point of reference, a marker, not a tomb like we have been told for millennium. It is proof that the people of the ancient world were truly more advanced than we are today. The new prime meridian of earth passes through Greenwich, England now. With unmitigated arrogance the Europeans move the true prime meridian of earth sometime after 1812 A.D.

The earth's orbit around the sun is not circular; it's elliptical. On July 3$^{rd}$ the earth is at its farthest point from the sun called the Aphelion about 94,000,000 miles and on December 31$^{st}$ the earth is at its closest point to the sun known as Perihelion about 91,300,000 miles. (94,000,000 + 91,300,000)/2 = 92,650,000 miles, this is the earth's average distance from the sun. What is most interesting is if the Great Pyramid's height of 482.7571 feet, is multiplied by 1,000,000,000 and then dividing that product by the number of feet in a mile, 5,280, one will have a working average of the earth's distance from the sun. This distance is 91,431,269 miles a difference of 1,218,731 miles or an accuracy of 98.7%, remarkable. The Great Pyramid's height relates to its perimeter as the radius of a circle does to its circumference. By dividing the average of the inner and outer perimeters of the Great Pyramid's base by twice its height, that yields 3.1417 or pi (3.1415). ( (3023+3043.8)/2)/ (2 (482.7571)) = 3.1417, a working approximation of pi.

The area of a face of the Great Pyramid is also the same as the square of its vertical height. If the slant height of a triangular facet of the Great Pyramid is divided by ½ times its base width, the result is 1.635. This fact indicates that the pyramid's design is in accordance with phi (1.618), also called the "Golden Number". $482.7571^2$ = ½ (755) (617.36267) and (617.36267)/ (1/2 (755)) = 1.635 A working approximation of the "Golden Number".

The "Golden Number" is a ratio of the sum of the length and width of a special rectangle divided by its length. The width and length of this special rectangle are as follows, 1,1, 2, 3, 5, 8,13, 21, 34, 55, 89, 144,... and so on, for example, (144+89)/ 144 = 1.61805556.

*These numbers are known as* Fibonacci Numbers or the Fibonacci Sequence and as the numbers in the sequence increase the ratio gets closer and closer to phi (1.618). Fibonacci's real name was Leonardo Pisano Bogollo an Italian who lived from 1170 A.D. to 1250 A.D. He traveled to Spain, where the knowledge was at the time in Western Europe, and studied Mathematics; upon his return to Italy he changed his name and plagiarized his book called the Liber Abaci. He is known today as one of the fathers of Algebra. He was not the only European to do this at the time. I will explain the flow of knowledge from Africa to the western world in later sections. This special rectangle is used as a border for priceless paintings, ancient and modern architecture and to display other priceless items.

This rectangular design is the most pleasing rectangle to the human eye. Even the pillars of the Taj Mahal are in accordance with this ratio. This ratio is also the sum of the lengths of the human body from feet to navel and navel to head divided by feet to navel. The ratio is 1.618. These measurements describe the most vertically proportional human form to the human eye. The average human has a ratio of about 1.64. This is not the only illustration of this ratio in the human form it is all over the body as described by the renaissance philosopher Nostradamus. The Golden Ratio is also present in shells, flowers and seeds, it is naturally occurring. Today, the basis of geography is the system of latitude and longitude.

Latitude and longitude measure the size of our planet and charts its surface with supreme accuracy. Most people think of this as an invention of the modern world because it requires a working knowledge of a higher form of mathematics such as spherical trigonometry. However, we find this exact knowledge incorporated into the interior and exterior measurements of the Great Pyramid.

The pyramid's perimeter is 3,023 feet, which is precisely equal to ½ of a minute of a degree of latitude at the equator, or 1:43,200 of the polar circumference of the earth. A measurement of the pyramid's perimeter, including the outer most sockets upon which it rests, yields a length of 3,043.8 feet, which is precisely equal to ½ of a minute of a degree of longitude at the equator, or 1:43,200 of the equatorial circumference of the earth. The entire pyramid rests on a platform, which is more than 755 feet in length and level to within 4/5 of an inch. The height of the pyramid plus the height of its base platform, 482.7571 feet, is equal to 1:43,200 of the polar radius of earth, or the distance from the center of the earth to the North Pole.

It should be noted here that the repetition of the formula 1:43,200 in the three measurements are intentional and relate to the size and shape of the earth. There are 360 degrees in a circle, 60 minutes in a degree and two ½ minutes in 1 minute. Simply put, 360 X 60 X 2 = 43,200. This means that if the Great Pyramid were 43,200 times its present size, it would fit perfectly inside the earth's Northern Hemisphere. These three basic measurements of the Great Pyramid, all on the same scale, represent the three essential geodetic values of our planet with a precision matched only with contemporary satellites or space shuttle surveys.

The Great Pyramid also has a footprint of 13 acres. It is centered on the 30th parallel, 1/3 of the way from the equator and 2/3 of the way from the North Pole. Placed at the geographical center of all the landmasses, it is oriented to the cardinal points of the compass. Keeping latitude and longitude in mind, the Great Pyramid is the focal point of this ancient grid map in which all the other ancient sites on earth are designed with respect to. This relationship the other ancient sites have with the Great Pyramid is found in the geometry of their location and construction. So, all the people of earth knew where the heart of the world resided and aligned their sacred sites accordingly. The very existence of the Great Pyramid implies an ancient global system in every aspect of the phrase.

Within the Great Pyramid is the so-called "King's Chamber" and "Queen's Chamber". These chambers have observation shafts that were cut through 200 feet of solid masonry to the outer surface of the pyramid. These shafts, in the King's chamber, which face in a northern and southern direction within one degree of accuracy, line up the northern celestial pole star (Polaris *today) and to the south the three stars*, specifically the eastern most star of Orion's Belt, (Osiris' Belt). The Queen's Chamber's southern observation shaft lines up with the star system Sirius; Sirius represents Osiris' wife, Isis. That's why it's called the Queen's chamber. This was done to mark the position of the earth relative to the star Isis (Sirius), to the star that does not move (the pole star) and the eastern most star, the Great Pyramid itself represented in the belt of Orion.

The latitude of the center of the King's Chamber is not considered at all because of its highly implausible implications. Its latitude is 29 degrees 58 minutes and 45.28 seconds N. The decimal degree value of this latitude is 29 degrees + 58' (1/60) + 45.28" (1/3600) = 29.9792458 degrees N. Calculations confirm that these digit locations of the decimal degree of the center of the King's Chamber are in the same location as the digits in the constant for the speed of light in a vacuum in meters per second, that is 299,792,458 m/s. Awesome. (Actually, for DMS to decimal degrees the calculations are accurate to within 99.99986157% but from decimal degrees to DMS, they are truly equal). It should be clear to you that the English and Metric systems of measure have their origins in Egypt, based on the evidence.

In that day, shall there be an altar to the Lord in the midst of the land of Egypt and a pillar thereof to the Lord (Isaiah 19:19). For many years, biblical scholars, believed that this verse is describing two different things, the altar and the pillar. However, in (Isaiah 19:20) the Bible states; And it shall be for a sign and for a witness unto the Lord of Hosts in the land of Egypt. The word "it" in this verse implies one object that is both an altar and a pillar unto the Lord. In the days of Isaiah, Egypt was divided into upper and lower Egypt. After World War I, the British went into Egypt to calculate the exact position of the original ancient border between the lands. The British discovered that the original border ran directly through the Great Pyramid of Giza. Consequently, the word "Giza" means "border" in Arabic. So, the Great Pyramid is the altar at the middle of Egypt and the pillar at the border that separates the two lands. Thus, the Great Pyramid is the altar of God and Egypt is the true Holy Land not Rome, Israel, Jerusalem or Mecca. So, it can be said that the Great Pyramid is

*Africa: It's True Role in the Ancient World* •

the ultimate expression of the combination of science and religion. The Egyptians combined that which should never be separated to honor the Lord of Hosts. How could these people be evil? How could this land be evil?

There are two other pyramids at Giza that make up the Pyramid Complex. The second largest pyramid, which is to the left of the Great Pyramid, if you are standing in front of the Sphinx in the foreground, and the smallest pyramid which is to the left of the other two. Together when viewed from the air, these pyramids are configured into an earthly duplication of the three stars that make up the belt of Orion. The distance between the pyramids is proportional to the lateral distance between the three stars that make up the belt. This means that if you had an aerial photo of the Pyramid Complex and a photo of the belt of Orion and superimposed them they would almost be a perfect superimposition today. Calculations confirm that the only time in the past that the distance between the three pyramids and the lateral distance between the three stars of the belt of Orion were proportional was in the year 10500 B.C.

The reason why they are not in a perfect superimposition today is because the stars have moved since the Complex's construction due to their regular rates. These calculations also confirm that these structures were built long before the Pharaohs Khufu, Khafre and Menaure were born (or the Dynasties go back further than the European is willing to admit). As far as I am concerned, these three pharaohs launched maintenance campaigns, maintaining the greatest of structures ever built so that their white lime stone shells and solid gold caps shined brightly again in order to build the pride, self-confidence and self-respect of the people of Africa.

When the Hoover Dam was completed in 1935 A.D., *the builders decided* to mark the time of completion by labeling spots on the ground that corresponded perfectly with the stars in the heavens on certain dates of the year so that if someone 3,000 years from now wanted to know when this structure was built, they could use the position of the stars to tell them. *This same procedure* was done for the Pyramid Complex at least 12,500 years ago according to the regular rates of the stars movements in the sky. Ironically, the Egyptologists will not acknowledge this evidence for it destroys their entire belief system and the European system of supremacy.

The most amazing fact about the Pyramid Complex is that these structures are mountains having a sum total footprint of 264 acres. The Complex rests on a man-made plateau, 131 feet above the Nile Delta, with an area of one square mile easily seen from everywhere. After learning about all these mathematical relationships incorporated in the Pyramid Complex, which barely scratches the surface of its mathematical and scientific complexities, I have come to the conclusion and realization that building this Complex was the easy part. All of this effort just to bury the pharaohs? This notion is laughable due in part to mathematics, science, and the purpose of the Valley of the Kings were all the Pharaohs are resting.

When the earth's crust shifted 2,244 miles to the south, it put the tropical Sahara into a desert zone now underneath at least 600 feet of sand. Again, sonar and radar mapping confirms this fact. It has been estimated that the Sahara Desert is only 8,000 years old. This desert phenomenon caused by the last polar shift covers an area larger than the continental United States (the lower 48, as it was called) and is the root of the Africans problems. In order to survive, our last great nation had to open its borders and trust outsiders around the year 4000 B.C.

I picked the year 4000 B.C. because the Europeans' picked this number covertly. Remember, he is the one who says history or his-story or creation started 6,000 years ago. This creation theory, ludicrous as the phrase sounds, with respect to its short time frame, has its only saving grace in the number 6,000 because it matches up with other evidence set down by the African. Moreover, it sounds like a secret hand shake or code among those who think like a Roman, Nazi, Skin Head, or Ku Klux Klan member. For in that year, the Africans educated a European man named

Socrates, who later educated a European man named Plato, who later educated a European man named Aristotle, who educated a European man named Philip, King of Macedonia who happened to be Alexander the Great's father.

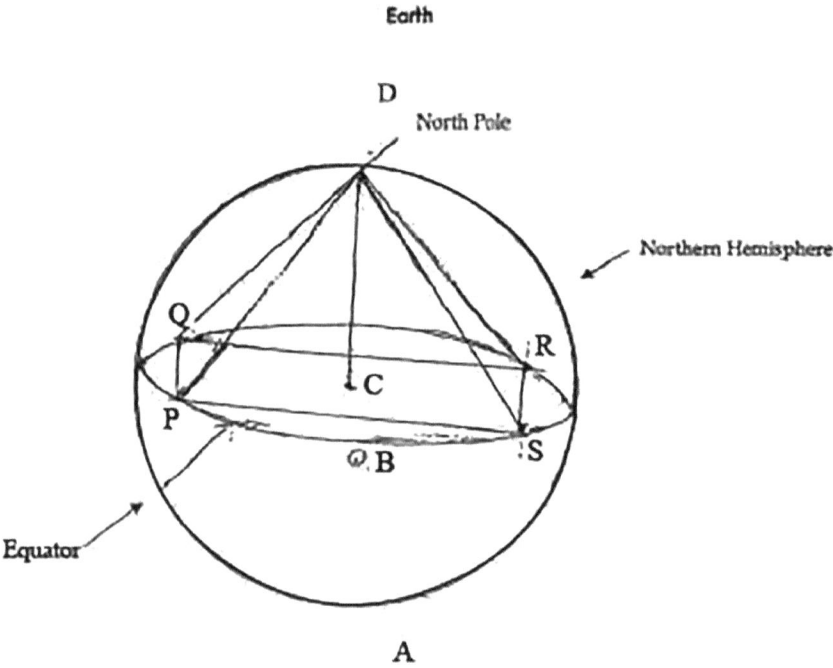

Circle "A" is the earth and Circle "B" is the Equator. Parallelogram PQRS is the base of the Great Pyramid, it is inscribed in Circle "B". Line segment CD is the Polar Radius of the earth, or the distance from the center of the earth to the North Pole. Line segments PQ, QR, RS, and SP are congruent and therefore a square. Thus, if the Great Pyramid was 43,200 times its present size, it would fit perfectly inside the earth's Northern Hemisphere or Southern Hemisphere for that matter.

| POLAR RADIUS | POLAR CIRCUMFERENCE VIA DEGREES LATITUDE AT THE EQUATOR | EQUALTORIAL CIRCUMFERENCE VIA DEGREES LONGITUDE AT THE EQUATOR |
|---|---|---|
| 482.7571 x 43,200 = 20,855,106.72 20,855,106.72/ 5.280 = 3,949.83 miles | 3,023 X 43,200 = 130,593,600 130,593,600/ 5,280 = 24,733.64 miles | 3,043.8 x 2 x 60 x 360 = 131,492,160 131,492,160/ 5,280 = 24,903.73 miles |

## The True Map of the Earth

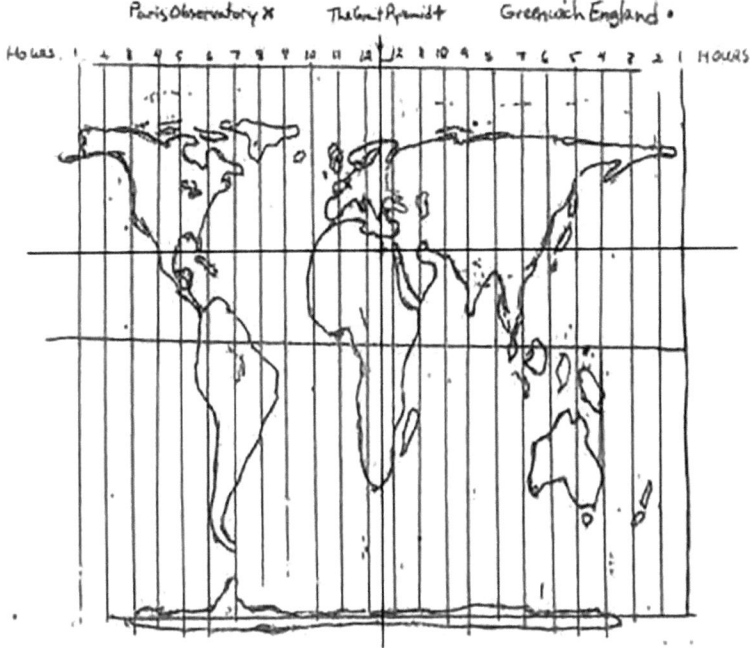

Note: The Great Pyramid is in the center of all the landmasses. It rests at the center of the longest **land** meridian, the true prime meridian and the longest **land** parallel on the globe, dividing the earth into equal quarters with respect to area. The Great Pyramid also lies at the center of gravity of all the continents. Which means that you can balance the map of the world on your finger under the Great Pyramid.

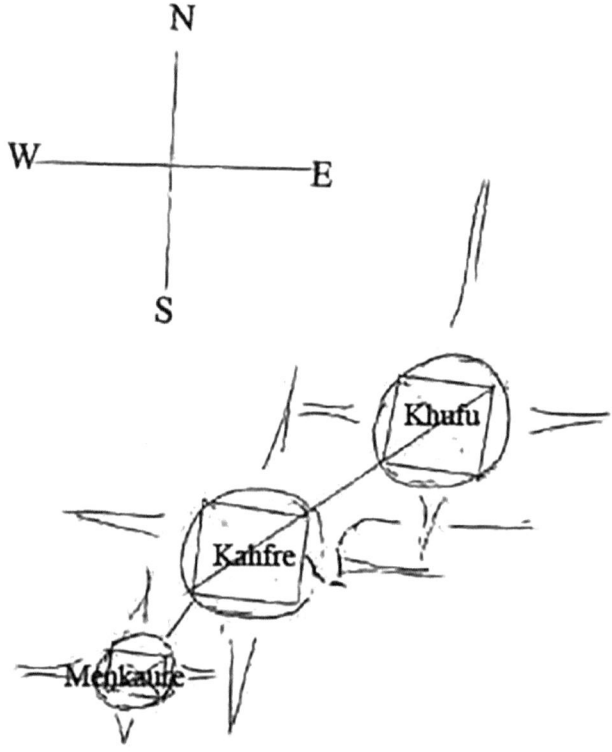

Together, when viewed from the air, the Pyramid Complex configures into an earthly duplication of the three stars that make up the belt of Orion (Osiris). The distance between the pyramids is proportional to the lateral distance between the three stars that make up the belt of Orion (Osiris). Calculations confirm that the only time in the past that the distance between the three pyramids and the lateral distance between the three stars were exactly proportional, i.e. a perfect superimposition, was in the year 10500 B.C. This marks their birth.

The Great Pyramid of Khufu, flanked by those of his sons, Khafre and Menkaure 10500 B.C.

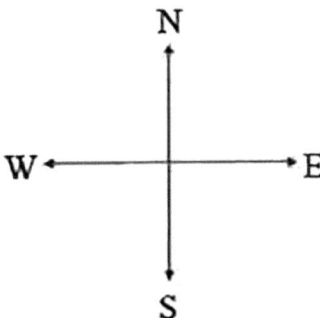

Menkaure Kahfre Khufu

The Sphinx is 265 feet long and 65 feet high. It is also almost the length of a football field and it is in this picture. Find it! Note the Great Pyramid is on the right.

# SECTION 5

# Attack of the Persians

The European says that the Persian Empire began 4,000 years ago with nomadic tribes eventually culminating into the largest empire the world has ever seen. In truth the largest empire the world has ever seen was Genghis Khan's Empire; his empire was five times larger than Persia. Still the Persia Empire was engineered with the first roads outside of Egypt, complete with kingdoms and gardens boasting two of the seven wonders of the ancient world, the Mausoleum and the Temple of Artemis.

All of the kingdoms of Persia had hot and cold running water, heating, air-conditioning, showers and flushing toilets, fountains and hanging gardens. The truth is, all of the technologies possessed by the Persians were learned in Egypt at the universities/kingdoms known today as Luxor/ Karnak, Memphis and Heliopolis before Cyrus the Great was born.

How else does a person become an engineer? If the reader is thinking "trial and error" then that particular person hoping to understand the applied works of mathematics needs the discipline, the bloodline to finish his/her commitments. They'd need countless eons to work within and the proper environment for contemplation. The only people on the earth who met all the requirements are the Africans. If education were irrelevant, then the barbarians that lived on the island of Britain, since before the end of the last ice age, would have made some technological and scientific leaps like the Persians supposedly did on their own. They clearly did not or by the time the warrior Queen Boudicca and her people had to fight the *injustices* of Nero's Roman armed forces in Britain, *at* least 9,000 years after the ice age in the year 60-61 A.D. to keep the Romans out of Britain. They would have been more of a formidable foe instead of lambs to the slaughter.

Then, sixty years later, Emperor Hadrian had a wall built across Great Britain, 73 miles in length to keep the barbarians in Scotland and out of the newly acquired Roman territory. Clearly, the Romans had access to something the barbarians to the north did not, which is the same miracle the Persians had access to years earlier. You have to understand that the human being is the only species on the earth that has to learn how to design and build anything and the European is hoping and praying that you forget this truth. This is a fact; the professionals who study the engineers of the animal kingdom will remind you of this fact.

The first ruler and unifier of Persia was Cyrus the Great, 580 B.C. to 530 B.C. He established the boundaries of the Persian Empire and took it to its glory. Cyrus conquered Babylon and freed the Jewish people. He also conquered Ionia, Greece (western Turkey today) and Egypt. Cyrus the Great was revered among his people and respected by his enemies.

Darius the Great, 550 B.C. to 486 B.C., also known as Darius I, was Cyrus the Great's cousin. Darius went on a campaign to expand the empire. He set his sights on Greece and built a floating bridge across the Bosporus. The Bosporus is a body of water that connects the Black Sea with the Aegean Sea and separates Europe from Asia or simply Greece from Persia. He attacked Greece in 490 B.C, with 25,000 troops, taking Macedonia by storm. But when he encountered the Greek military genius, Themistocles and his 10,000 troops at the Battle of Marathon, the Persians lost but some of the Persians set sail to take Athens.

The Athenians who just defended the sovereignty of Marathon sent a runner named Pheidippides back to Athens to warn of the attack. Pheidippides ran the full 26 miles nonstop and carried out his duties then dropped dead of heat exhaustion. Why didn't he just ride a horse? Anyway, what we know as the marathon commemorates his heroic run from Marathon to Athens. The Persians were thwarted before making it to Athens and eventually retreated back to Persia. On his way back, Darius the Great dies trying to stop the first rebellion in Egypt.

Darius' son, Xerxes, 519 B.C. to 465 B.C. finished his father's work and quelled the Egyptian rebellion. Xerxes also wanted to take Greece to expand his empire into present day Europe. He devised a plan to attack Greece from two fronts this time one by land and the other by sea. Xerxes built another floating bridge across the Bosporus. This bridge is wider than his father's so he could take a larger army across. An army of 300,000 troops, most of which were on horseback went across the floating bridge and attacked the Greeks at the city/state called Thermopylae.

Thermopylae had a narrow path that only allowed one chariot through at a time. One side of the path was mountainous and the other side was the Aegean Sea. Themistocles, an Athenian general and statesman, left an army of only 6,000 Spartan troops (pawns) to defend the land front at Thermopylae. These 6,000 troops are the inspiration of that movie "300" released in 2007 A.D. Themistocles knew he would have problems fighting the Persians on land so he cut his losses and concentrated on the Persian navy.

Themistocles had a false traitor lie to the Persian King Xerxes about the strength of the Greek Navy and where they were most vulnerable. The Persians bought it unaware they were sailing into a trap. The Persian Navy had 700 ships laced with 150,000 warriors, outnumbering the Greeks 2 to 1. The trap was sprung in the narrow straits of Salamis where the much larger ships of the Persians would have a difficult time maneuvering. The Greeks rammed the much larger and slower Persian ships, destroying nearly all of them in the straits while they only lost forty of their own. The rest of the Persian ships retreated home to Persia. Meanwhile, the Persian army defeated the Greeks at Thermopylae, taking it and then burning Athens to the ground. Though the Europeans would have you believe otherwise, the Athens before Alexander the Great and for that matter all of

Greece was of wood and thatch buildings and dung style homes, not of the huge marble structures we know today as Ancient Greece. The reason? The Greeks had not been taught on a massive scale by the Egyptians yet. This is the great secret of the ages that I will reveal soon enough. Nonetheless, because of the loss of Athens, the ungrateful Greeks voted against Themistocles. He was later ostracized by the Greek Senate and forced to become one with an enemy he lived most of his life trying to destroy. He would never see Greece again.

Artaxerxes, son of Xerxes and grandson of Darius the Great, lived from 465 B.C. to 425 B.C. During his lifetime, the Greeks went into Egypt to support a second rebellion against the Persians. These conditions allowed the Greeks to enter into Egypt to fight as mercenaries against a common enemy. Some of the Greeks took advantage of this opportunity and went to school to study the Arts and Sciences. One of these students went by the name Socrates. Artaxerxes had to leave his building projects in Persia to launch a military attack on Egypt and the Greeks who now occupied the Egyptian capital city of Memphis. The Persians finally kicked the Greeks out, bringing Egypt back under Persian rule again.

This was the last great victory of Persia. After Artaxerxes' death in 425 B.C., a power vacuum occupied the throne of Persia, creating an international conflict lasting seventy-eight years, giving Greece and Egypt time to regroup. Darius III, who is a distant relative of Artaxerxes, finally acquires full power and is declared ruler of Persia in 336 B.C. He will forever be remembered as the king who lost an empire.

*Africa: It's True Role in the Ancient World* •

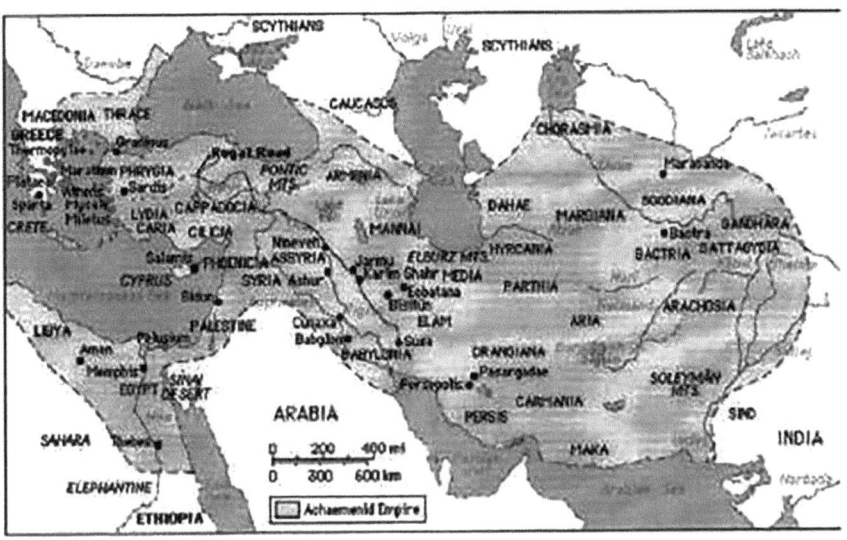

This is the extent of the Persian Empire. The European distorted the time line to hide his academic dependence on the African after Alexander's invasion of Persia.

## SECTION 6

# The Truth about Alexander the Great

Alexander the Great is well known throughout the historic and academic communities. For centuries scholars have debated as to what makes Alexander the Great so great. What made Alexander great is that he realized that the source of the knowledge that he had received was in Africa, to the south of the Mediterranean Sea. And when Africa needed help in their third rebellion against the Persians, Alexander knew that the timing was right for him to become an African patriot.

He inspired an army of 40,000 to help him rescue the African as a gesture of good faith in hopes that the African would share their knowledge with the European and finally bring the European into the light of humanity. This is what made Alexander great. What is most interesting is that very few common people know of the magnitude of his kingdom.

Alexander was born of Philip, King of Macedonia; he attempted to conquer the occupying forces known as the Persians. This invading army stretched from Africa to the south to Macedonia (Greece) in the north to Pakistan in the east. Alexander had something very rare in Greece at that time:—an education. Alexander was taught by his father and the philosopher Aristotle, who was taught by Plato, who was taught by Socrates. Alexander was taught the philosophies and principles of life that were laid down by the people who were around long enough to have paid attention to those types of rhythms, the great Africans.

Alexander learned of mathematics, engineering, astronomy, astrology, medicine, physics and the epic nature of the African. He was so intrigued and inspired by the Africans that when he found out that a third rebellion was going on in Africa against the Persians, he gathered an army of 40,000 Greek soldiers and began his adventures into history. Alexander, the new king of Greece, as of 336 B.C. fought his way through the straights of Istanbul knowing the only reason for his success was that more than half of the Persian King's heavily armed navy was in Africa fighting the third Egyptian rebellion. Alexander moved through Turkey, then Syria destroying the Persian naval ports as he advanced.

When he arrived in Jordan, he defeated the armies of Darius III an army three times the size of his own. Darius III, King of Persia, was allowed to escape back east into the heart of his kingdom. At this point, Alexander had considered himself king of Persia and allotted his Persian prisoners the same positions and status they enjoyed under Darius III. Meanwhile, Alexander the Great did the unthinkable. Instead of hunting Darius III down and capturing him before he could get dug in, regroup and develop a new weapon plus put an end to a 210-year long war as a great commander and chief would and should have, Alexander left an army of 20,000 there in Jordan to continue the battle as he, his right-hand man, General Ptolemy and the other half of his soldiers ventured the rest of the way to Africa. There must have been something in Africa that was more important to Alexander than ending this 210-year long war. What is most interesting is that no one questioned his authority after this unprecedented move. Also, notice that Alexander and his forces traveled by land and not by sea. This is because they burned all of their own ships during their civil war called the Peloponnesian wars, 80 years earlier.

As Alexander entered the Sinai Peninsula, heading due west, he was guided by a light in the distance that glowed brightly in the sunlight during the daytime and brightly at night in the moonlight. This phenomenon mesmerized and frightened his followers but not Alexander. He had studied in detail about this phenomenon on manuscripts from his teacher. He knew the light was the reflection from the tallest and largest complex in the world, the Pyramid Complex. The glow was from the white limestones incasing the pyramids and their solid gold caps. The Complex stood a full 613 feet above the Nile Delta and covered an area of 264 acres. It was easily seen from everywhere.

When Alexander arrived in Africa, he breathed a sigh of relief. He knew he was among people greater than himself. He also knew that these people could answer all of his burning questions about his success and what it meant for the war. Alexander spent six weeks in Africa on a quest during this war. This is like General McArthur taking a six-week vacation in the Bahamas during WWII. In other words, this is unheard of. Most scholars say Alexander spent a full six months in Africa during this war. This is even more evidence in Africa's favor as the true Holy Land and its unrivaled importance and significance to Alexander the Great.

Considering the many locations Alexander traveled to in the Nile Valley plus the fact that he had to kick the Persians out first, the six-month time frame is much more feasible and creditable than the supposed six weeks. Nevertheless, Alexander spent this time paying homage to Heru's black image in the Great Sphinx, the Pyramid Complex, the four statues of Ramses the Great, the kingdoms of Luxor/Karnak, Memphis and Heliopolis where he learned what a kingdom/university should look like and how its infrastructure should be designed and built. (These kingdoms are the world's very first universities plus the very word luxury has its roots in the kingdom called Luxor).

He was also allowed to view many of the honored dead of Africa in the Valley of the Kings. This valley is a distance of 1,324 miles south of the Nile Delta. Alexander also went to the desert Oasis located in the northwest corner of Egypt where the Siwa Temple or University stood. This temple lies due west on the same parallel the Pyramid Complex rests on. This parallel is the border between the two lands. He almost died of thirst during the trip. This trek that Alexander took to Siwa is where college fraternities and sororities get the phrase "crossing the burning sands." This phrase describes the trials and tribulations an individual endures when on line as a Neophyte for at least six weeks in an attempt to join the organization. Whether they know it or not, the fraternities and sororities during their pledge season are simulating or reenacting the trials and tribulations of Alexander while he was in Africa. The word Neophyte is an African word that means new or rookie.

Alexander asked his burning questions here at Siwa. This is where he was transformed and transmogrified into an avenging angel. He was told he was both man and god. He was told that he was now a pharaoh and to go complete the mission to destroy the invaders and make his way into Asia and then you can take your place by the African's side. (Note: it was more important to Alexander to become pharaoh than it was to be King of Greece, King of Persia or capture his mortal enemy, King Darius III).

To prove he made it to Asia, Alexander was to bring back the Opium flower, for it only grew in Southeast Asia at that time. Alexander was given African doctors who treated his wounded with opiates; they used opium to soothe pain before and after surgery. The opiates were also used to soothe the painful feet and legs of the troops so they could march the 22,000 miles they eventually covered. Alexander is the one who brought opium to India where it still flourishes today. Before Alexander left Africa, he surveyed the region where his kingdom would be built. He then told General Ptolemy to stay in Africa and aid in the rebellion on this side of the front while Alexander flanked the Persians from the other side to capture the Persian king, King Darius III.

He also said to Ptolemy, "If I die before I return to build my kingdom, I leave it to you to make sure my kingdom is built on this spot in this land of Africa and that my body be mummified in the great traditions of the people so that I can also inspire generations forever."

Alexander returned to meet up with his army. They beat the Persians and captured Darius III but the cost of this victory was Alexander's life. The army of Greece, while taking the body of Alexander back to Macedonia to be buried, was intercepted by the Ptolemy who brought Alexander's body back to Africa as he was commanded. No one questioned his authority on this unprecedented matter either. Alexander's body was mummified and placed in the Alexandrian Museum. This 256-foot domed palace was built by the Africans for this great pharaoh and was designed to hold the artifacts of the world's past with Alexander's mummified body as its centerpiece.

They built the University of Alexandria complete with 400 lecture halls that were domed and enclosed, observatories, science laboratories, hospitals, engineering laboratories, a zoo with an aquarium, green houses, dormitories, apartment buildings (condominiums), a gymnasium, a stadium for soccer, clock towers and a library as its centerpiece. This library was a 300-foot cube of smoked glass that had the capacity to hold 1,000,000 consolidated African manuscripts stacked neatly on endless shelves with each of its thirty floors fully staffed. The library also had the ability to hold over 1,000 people and the reading machines they used to accommodate them comfortably.

These reading machines were designed like the weaver machine used to make clothes. The reader would sit down in the machine, place one rolling pin in a clasp and the other rolling pin in a clasp below the first. The reader would then open the pins, press the foot pedal up and down and the rolling pins would roll for the reader to read the manuscript. The next building to be completed was the palace of the Ptolemy. It was said to have two towers, one was 365 feet tall the other was 28 feet shorter to represent sun and moon plus, an east and west wing that stretched one mile along the coast of the eastern harbor of the kingdom. There was also an additional 4,000 luxurious palaces with 4,000 baths the size of Olympic swimming pools to house and maintain the peace of mind as well as encourage the physical, mental and spiritual growth of the professors, master teachers, engineers, architects, navigators, craftsmen, artisans, masons and librarians of the University of Alexandria.

This is when the teacher lived like professional athletes do today. It should be noted that these manuscripts are now called the Classics by the European since his Renaissance Period. Thus, this period between Alexander's death and the rise of the Roman Empire became known as the Classical Period to the Europeans. Fortunately, it should also be noted that the music of the European Renaissance Period is known as classical music. It is the music of higher consciousness. It is not a coincidence that classical music and the classical period have the same first name. Classical music comes from the classical period performed in Egypt before and during the 32$^{nd}$ Dynasty.

As it later was with the Roman palaces, each of the buildings of the Kingdom of Alexandria were masterpieces of craftsmanship, art and architecture with marble mosaic floors, and precious metals and jewels lacing the walls and ceilings. Remember that up to this time the Egyptians had over 3,000 years of experience building with stone, brick and wood as well as extracting precious metals and jewels from deep within the earth according to the European. The rest of the kingdom was built behind the downtown area and university in the form of what is now known as colonial style homes, brownstones, split-levels and business buildings for the 1,000,000 residents and their comfort. These colonial style homes and split-levels were also designed with porches and patios. The crowning jewel of this beach front property was the combination of a man-made double harbor and lighthouse. This double harbor had and still has to this very day an area of about 10 square miles and was capable of holding ships 400 feet long, the longest ships in the world at that time, ships specifically designed for the Alexandrian harbor. This harbor was built with waterproof concrete to calm the rough waters of the Mediterranean Sea for the safe port of these mega ships. These mega ships made port at least 200 times daily. That's twice as many ships entering the New York harbor today. Any ship longer than 125 feet and wider than 25 feet could only make port in Alexandria.

At the entrance of the double harbor stood the 6th wonder of the Ancient World, a 440-foot-tall Lighthouse with a light that the Europeans say could be seen 200 miles out to sea. Plus, if that beam of light were focused on a ship it would set that ship ablaze up to 35 miles away.

This kingdom was the very definition of a downtown. It was complete with buildings constructed out of the finest marble ranging from 20 to 440 feet tall or as tall as all the buildings in downtown Detroit, save the three tallest ones. The three tallest would be the circular cylinder of the Renaissance Center, the Comerica Building and the Penobscot Building. No building was to be taller than the mathematical masterpiece known today as the Pyramid Complex whose height is a product of its design, 482.7571 feet. Moreover, downtown Alexandria was as expansive as downtown Chicago or New York City's Manhattan Island.

Alexandria was the largest and greatest learning center that the world has ever seen. This was a kingdom that was truly of the people, by the people and for the people. Alexandria was the zenith of civilization, period. A utopia was designed and built for Alexander the Great. The Europeans deny none of this. They dummy the kingdom down to just a library and declare it a product of Greek innovation, hoping you don't ask questions, let alone learn about his version of the story. If you don't ask questions then the European can deny that this is where he received his education so that later he could build his first kingdoms.

These are the kingdoms the world knows today as Ancient Greece and Ancient Rome respectively. The European also denies how long he had access to this library, the length of time the Greeks and the Africans were married, so to speak, and that this marriage ever existed in the first place. By the way, the European version of this story is called Hellenism or the Hellenistic period. Fortunately, it follows that both the Classical and Hellenistic periods are code words for the gift of African knowledge according to the evidence.

The European also denies the type of energy source used to make this Lighthouse a wonder of the Ancient World. The Lighthouse was tall but it was not the tallest building in the world at that time. The Great Pyramid still held that title up until the construction of the 986-foot- tall Eiffel Tower in 1889 A.D. So, the Lighthouse was not a wonder of the world due to its height. The Lighthouse was a wonder of the world because of its light. Then the European says that this light that could be seen by him 200 miles out to sea had a source of some wood or oil burning fire at the focus point of a huge parabolic mirror. The critical thinker knows that neither wood nor oil can produce a light luminescent enough or intense enough to be seen 200 miles out to sea no matter how huge the parabolic mirror is and still be safe enough for people to function.

So, if you can see a light of fire 200 miles away, you wouldn't go there because that would mean that the whole city was on fire. Yet, everyone went to Alexandria. Moreover, wood was scarce in Egypt; it would not have been used as a fuel source at all during the lifespan of the Lighthouse.

The Kingdom of Alexandria had heating and air conditioning, hot and cold running water, showers and flushing toilets, water fountains and hanging gardens. This is everything we are told the Romans had and they had it much, much later. The Romans pressurized their plumbing system with aqueducts, running water down-hill from a water source in the mountains. Egypt does not have mountains to run an aqueduct from. So, the question begs, how did they pressurize their plumbing system?

The Egyptians pressurized their plumbing system with water towers that used electrical devices to pump the water to the top of the tower to pressurize the kingdom. Buildings in the kingdom taller than the water towers had their own water storage tanks on the top floor to pressurize the building. Alexandria, Egypt is also strategically located between two water sources, the Mediterranean Sea and Lake Mariout.

Electricity is one thing the Romans did not have. Not because it was not in use but because they did not understand its principles. These principles require time and wisdom. Wisdom comes with age and the Romans were not old enough mentally to make use of it. To make a long story short, there is no other source of light produced by man that is luminescent enough or intense enough to be seen the distance from Detroit to Chicago. The only energy source luminescent enough or intense enough to be seen 200 miles out to sea is electricity.

What's more is there were one hundred-fifty modern medical procedures performed in Alexandria, including brain surgery, dental surgery, eye surgery, bladder surgery, cosmetic surgery, bone setting and caesarean section, performed surprisingly with the same surgical instruments used today. These ancient surgical instruments were supposedly discovered after the modern surgical instruments were already produced and in use.

It turns out that all the surgical instruments that a modern-day surgeon would be familiar with are engraved on the walls of the temple of Komobo dedicated to the true father of medicine the multi-genius Imhotep of the 3rd Dynasty. The medical operation known as caesarean section or c-section as it is called today was named after Queen Cleopatra's son Caesarean, son of Julius Caesar. This operation was performed in Africa as a common medical procedure countless times before Caesareans birth. It became famous when it was performed on Cleopatra because she was unable to give birth naturally.

It was the first time the European was exposed to this procedure. (Eye, dental and brain surgery cannot be performed without anesthesia, antiseptic, magnifying glasses and a constant and focused light source so the surgeon can see). You have to understand, a good surgeon during the American Civil War was a fast surgeon because the European had nothing to stop the pain and no medical skills to fix the body in 1865 A.D. so amputation was the order of the day.

The eye surgery in Alexandria was done for the purposes of removing the lenses due to cataracts. What people don't realize is that after the lenses are removed, the patient will need artificial lenses to take the place of the damaged natural ones. These artificial lenses are called glasses today. There is also evidence that the brain surgery patients actually survived after the surgery due to the fact that their skulls showed signs of extensive healing.

The European says that the Great Library was completed in 298 B.C., why does he even mention it at all? Nevertheless, the mummified body of the King of Greece remained on foreign soil until Emperor Augustus of Rome took Alexander's body back to Europe. This was a direct violation of Alexander's orders.

## Alexander the Great

Alexander's epic battle with Darius III before he entered Africa to be declared a god.

*Africa: It's True Role in the Ancient World* •

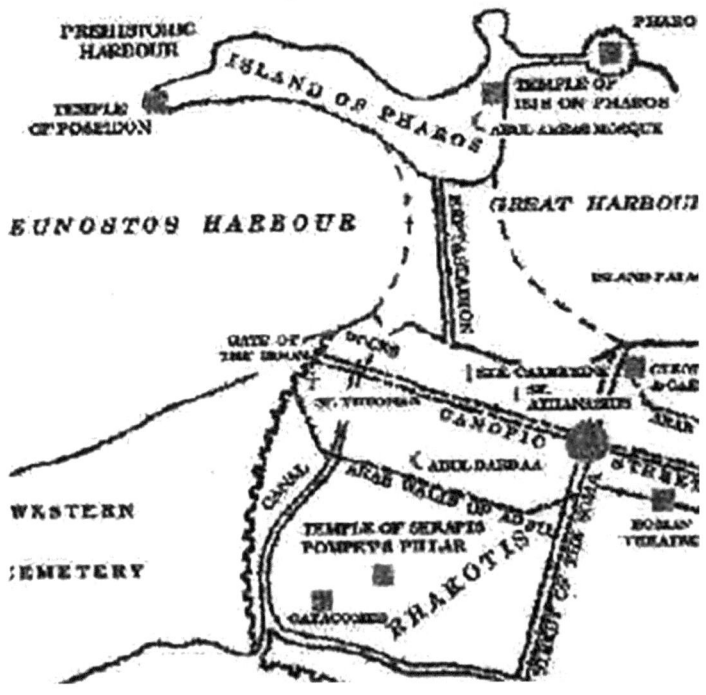

Scholars say that the oldest part of Alexander's kingdom is the causeway called Heptastadion. The European will have you believe that the area between the dashed lines is sedimentary deposits over time. Well, if this is true (and it's not) then science should be able to prove its age with the rate of deposit. The critical thinker knows that the island of Pharos and the African mainland have been there for countless millions of years, well before they were given names and all of a sudden the sediment decides that it can't attach itself to the landmasses without that man made causeway. Then when it connects itself it does it with a seamless, flawless semi circle on both sides. Amazing! This is an example of the engineering genius of the African, reclaiming 960 acres of land with water proof concrete. How could a city of stone be built on sediment? This not only includes the ancient city but the modern city that rests there today. Even the Romans had water proof concrete. Who do you think taught them?

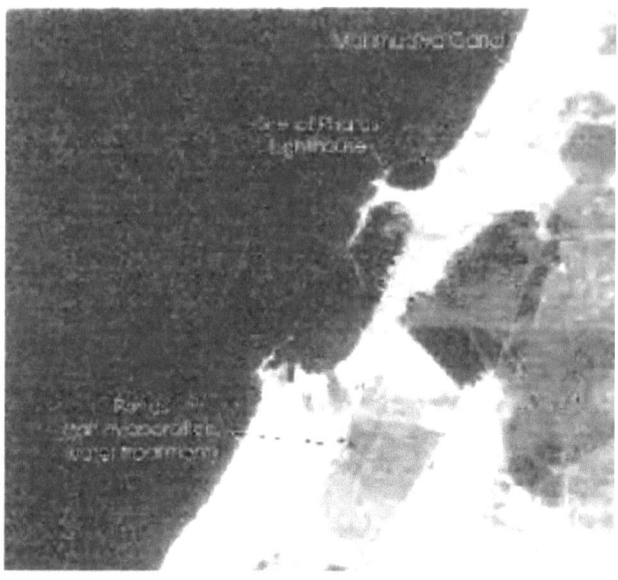

This is Alexander's Kingdom with 960 acres (1.54 square miles) of man made land connecting the mainland of Africa to the Island of Pharos. This man made land also separates the Eastern Harbor from the Western Harbor.

# SECTION 7

# An African Mystery System: Electrical Engineering

What does it take to make electricity? Everything needed to produce electricity comes from the ground. Electricity is produced by spinning a magnet's north and south poles in a clockwise or counterclockwise manner inside a helix coil of copper or gold wire. Both can be fashioned with heat and made into a wire that can be wrapped into a helix coil pattern like an Archimedes Screw.

This screw design is so old that it was used to pull water out of the African's gold and copper mines. Today a turbine is used to spin the magnet inside a copper coil of wire. A waterfall through a tube is the source of the energy that makes the turbine spin, which spins the magnet inside the helix coil, therefore, producing electricity. If the Archimedes Screw can be used to move water out of mines, then water can be used to spin an Archimedes Screw, which could be used in reverse to make electricity by pushing water passed it.

The ebb and flow of the Mediterranean Sea or high tide and low tide, as they are called today, are created by the Sun and Moon's dance across the sky. This causes an imbalance in the water sources surface. This process, which is in perfect harmony with the environment and the surroundings, can be used to create a waterfall through a tube.

The over flowing water, as it rises, will be sent through the tube to an Archimedes Screw where the magnet sits inside a helix of gold or copper wire in a plane perpendicular to the sides of the coil walls.

Water weighs 62.4 pounds per cubic foot and has an enormous amount of potential energy. As the water rises over the top of the tubes, the overflow is sent into a man-made bay where more tubes exist so when the tide is low, the man-made bay will take the process over until high tide returns again. This is genius at work. Here we have a continuous, renewable energy source described here, produced by the gravity of the Sun and Moon. The wire at the top of the coil goes in one direction and the other wire at the bottom of the coil expands in the opposite direction. These wires meet wherever you desire in length. Make a point of discontinuity, passing the water through the tube that causes the Archimedes Screw to spin, which in turn spins the magnet inside the helix coil of gold wire. The electricity will pass through the wire in one direction like slot cars in a race. One side of the discontinuity will be positive and the other side will be negative. When you bring the wires closer together, you can watch the slot cars jump the gap. Eureka! We have electricity. Later on, we can figure out how many slot cars to put on the track, "amperage," what kind of energy level they will carry, "voltage", how intense we want the light of the Lighthouse to be, "resistance", and then we can use a huge parabolic mirror for focus.

Note that if you mastered the art and principles of electricity, you wore a snake on your head. A snake (Asp) is just as deadly as electricity and if you could not control the Asp and respect its potential then it would kill you just as electricity would. Also, the snake, when mobile, is in the shape of the sine wave or sine function, representing electric current or oscillation. The snake is the Egyptian symbol for electricity.

*Africa: It's True Role in the Ancient World* •

## The Light House of Alexandria

The 440 foot tall 6th Wonder of the World, the Lighthouse of Alexandria, in Egypt. It was not a wonder because of its height, it was a wonder because of its light. A light that the European says he could see 200 miles out to sea. It was also a weapon

## The Truth

The European says he could see the light from the Lighthouse 200 miles out to sea. Mathematics and Science says he could see the light 27 miles out to sea before it dropped below the horizon.

ds—Straight line distance to the horizon
h—Height
r—Radius of the earth

$$d_s = \sqrt{h(2r_p + h)}$$

dc—Curved distance along the planet's surface to the horizon at sea level

$$d_c = r_p \cos^{-1}\left(\frac{r_p}{r_p + h}\right)$$

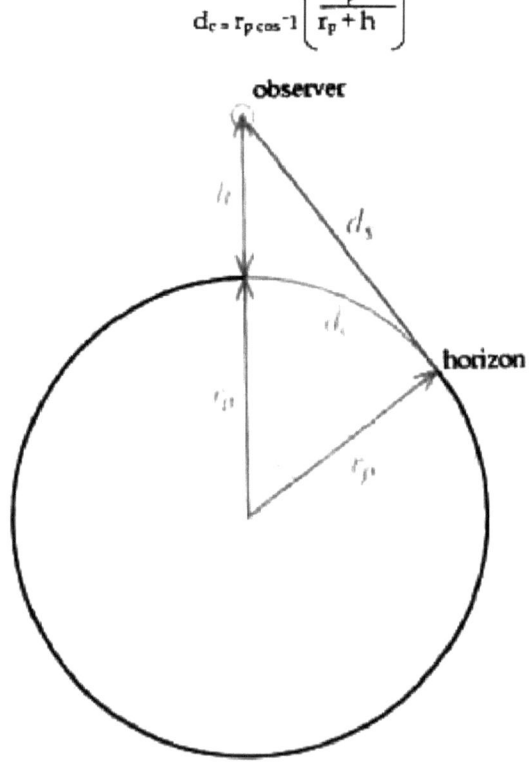

# Africa: It's True Role in the Ancient World

In order for the European to see the light 200 miles away as he says, the light envelope itself would have a radius of 5 miles in height. Not impossible. Light spreads as it leaves its source like a light from a flashlight on a wall. But like a light from a flashlight, the further you are away from the wall, the less intense the light is. If the European could see the light from that far away, then the light would have to have the intensity of the Sun i.e. setting ships on fire up to 35 miles away. Still, to see a light the distance from downtown Detroit to Monroe City would have to be of electricity. It is also interesting to note that if an individual were standing at the top of the Lighthouse that person could definitely see the curvature of the earth at sea level at the horizon.

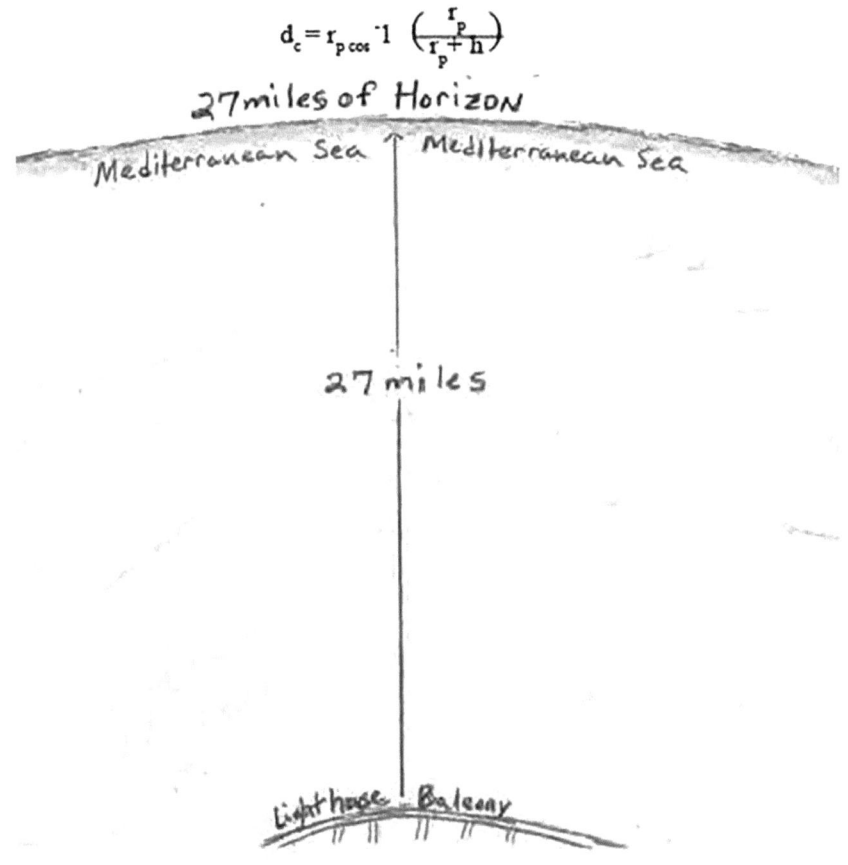

The distribution of power will be constant between the Mediterranean Sea and the man made bay. This power supply is infinite given maintenance it is environmentally sound.

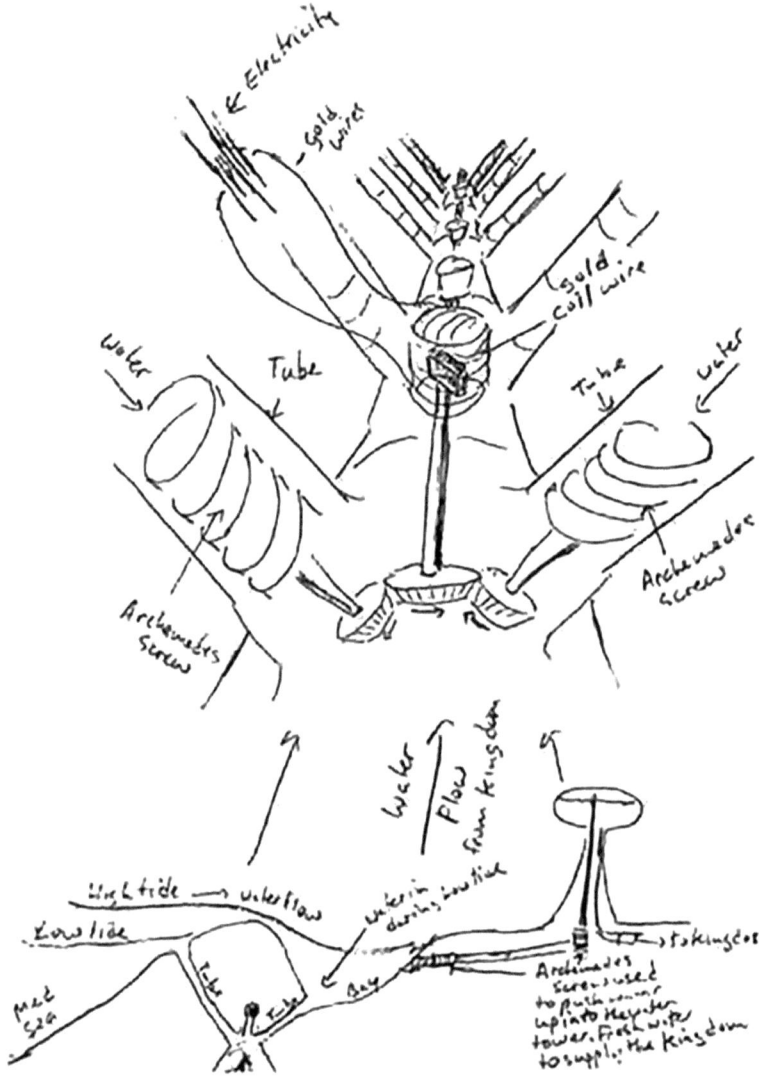

# SECTION 8

# The Past

When the Alexandrian Kingdom was completed, the Ptolemaic Family, the 32$^{nd}$ Dynasty, was the first appointed white family of Europeans to mate with the Africans in the form of the last black dynasty of Egypt, the 30th Dynasty. While the Greeks first Bible, the Europeans first Bible, the Septuagint version of the Bible, was being diligently written, compared and revised from the original Egyptian text, known as Per-Em-Heru, one of the members of the Ptolemaic bloodline of pharaohs asked an African named Mer-enjiuti, who's also known as Manetho, Professor of History and Librarian of the University of Alexandria, to write down the history of his great land, its nations and its great people for prosperity.

He wrote five large volumes on the subject. He wrote down the godhood of man that existed on earth before the last polar shift. This polar shift caused the indigenous people of earth to adapt to great changes in their society. These changes included the loss of a great continent outside of Africa and more than half of their species. This polar shift is also responsible for the extinction of the Saber Tooth Tiger species, the Woolly Mammoth species and all the other mega mammals that thrived at the time of the ice age, as well as their food. It also marks the end of the ice age around the year 9500 B.C. This polar shift is the real reason that the people of earth built the Pyramid Complex. They are not tombs as we have been told but structures that will never fall down in an equally cataclysmic earth movement.

The pyramids were also built to mark the time when the people of earth reached godhood, to remind future generations that it is possible to be at this level of achievement given time and the right state of mind. The people of earth built them just in case things became worse than they already were, just in case we forget ourselves, like today. It turns out that this polar shift also left Africa in a desert zone. A desert that completely covered northern Africa about 4,500 years after the pyramids were constructed, about 6000 B.C. or 8,000 years ago. One more thing, the majority of the mammals before the Ice Age were at least twice as large as the mammals of today.

What about man? Shaquille O'Neil is a 7 foot 3-inch-tall mammoth that only looks tall when he is around other people. Yet unlike most people his size, he is proportional. Plus, eighty-five percent of the NBA, the NFL, and the MLB are Africans and these brainless athletes are depicted and worshipped as gods today. Can you imagine how tall and massive we were when the grass grew in the Sahara? Extrapolation says we were on average twice as tall and massive as we are today, just like all the other mammals were.

Yes, we were gods and the Pyramid Complex is supposed to remind us of that truth. Furthermore, like all the other mammals, we also adapted and shrank in size to compensate for our new environment yet still maintaining our intellect. All the while the European was in a cave in Europe on all fours waiting for the ice to melt, still exiled from humanity by Heru, the one whose image is on the Sphinx.

The Greeks did not believe in this godhood stuff despite the evidence. So, they concentrated on the human dynasties. These dynasties were the Dynasties of Egypt. The Dynasties of Egypt consisted of thirty distinct dynasties confirmed by the professor of history, Mer-enjuiti. Mer-enjuiti also said that the first dynasty started over 5,700 years before his time. The European says that the Alexandrian Library was completed in the year 298 B.C. when in actuality, this is probably the year Mer-enjuiti was asked or when he finished his work. If you add 298 years to 5,700 it equals 6,000 years.

*Africa: It's True Role in the Ancient World* •

This number will bring the timeline to zero, or Jesus' birth, life, and murder. Remember, he is the pivot point in Western time.

Now, if I add another 2,000 years to that sum, I get 8,000 years since the first of the 30 dynasties started or 2,000 A.D., which is today. This is 3,000 years earlier than the supposed 3000 B.C. history of Egypt that we have been told for centuries. Mer-enjiuti also provided the world with the length of time the 30 dynasties ruled earth. That time period was 2,889 years. So, if you take 2,889 from 8,000 you will get 5,111 years. Now for the shocker, take 2,000 years from 5,111 years and you will be at the number 3,111. That's 3111 B.C. because that 2,000 you took away is all the years after Jesus' murder.

In other words, Alexander the Great, first appointed pharaoh of Africa, was alive a lot closer to 3111 B.C. than 298 B.C. It can also be assumed that his kingdom in Africa was completed in at least 50 years.

Ptolemy I, the second appointed European pharaoh of Africa, was Alexander's number one general during the Persian War. To reiterate about Ptolemy I, that's the family that mated with the last black dynasty of Africa, the 30th Dynasty. Again, no discernable gaps exist between the period of the thirty dynasties and the Ptolemaic rule and together they consumed over 6,000 years.

This date of 3111 B.C. implies too many things, such as the Kingdom of Alexandria stood for at least 3,111 years before Christ and 415 years after his murder. That's at least 3,500 years. Incredible. Plus, the first of the thirty dynasties had to have started around the year 6000 B.C. or 8,000 years ago and not 5,000 years ago as we have been told. Ironically, these dates are consistent with the time the tropical Sahara became a desert as confirmation by sonar and radar mapping. This is a testament to African ingenuity and longevity as civilization pushed up against the last lifeline in North Africa, the Nile River. The dates for the Persian War as reported by the European are grossly inaccurate because Alexander ended the Persian threat of tyranny.

This also implies that the European has the distinction of being part of the longest lasting single dynastic period, the Ptolemaic bloodline. Many European scholars for the purpose of separating Europe from Africa reject this distinction. This number also implies that the European had access to the University of Alexander for more than 3,111 years before Christ. This is when and where he received his education from the African. It further implies that Ancient Greece and Ancient Rome are nothing more than classroom assignments handed out by the Africans.

Still, there is another reason why they reduced the time period of Alexander's Kingdom by a factor of 10. It should be noted that there were 19 Pharaohs ruling during this time, the time of the 32nd Dynasty. They are the 12 Pharaohs named Ptolemy and the 7 Queens name Cleopatra. If we subtract Queen Cleopatra VII's age of 39 years from the 3,111, then divide that result by 18 Pharaohs, we would get the average lifespan of a European Pharaoh at that time. Simply put, $(3,111-39)/18 = 170$ years. The European never lived better at any time period or any where else on earth than when they lived in Africa. Their lifespan, while living in Africa, is a testament to our way, the African way of life.

Now, if I add the 2,000 years back to the 3,111 years I'll get 5,111 years ago. Remember the European says creation started 6,000 years ago? Well, 6,000 minus 5,111 is 889 years. What the European is really saying about this number 6,000 is that he was educated for the first time that many years ago. Also, the first European to be educated was Socrates (or Pythagoras because he was born 90 years before Socrates, 560 B.C. to 480 B.C., according to the European and Pythagoras is known to have traveled and studied in Egypt according to the Masonic Order.) This means that Socrates, Plato, and Aristotle never knew each other personally. They only knew each other through each other's work and travels because there are at most, 889 years between Socrates and Aristotle and neither of the three lived past 80 years old.

Furthermore, Aristotle tutored Alexander the Great. The philosopher Hippocrates, (Hippocratic oath for physicians) who also lived some- time between Socrates and Aristotle, declared that he was a child of the teachings of the multi-genius Imhotep (Greek name Asclepius and worshipped as a Greek God) who lived in Egypt during the 3rd Dynasty at least 4,400 years before Hippocrates according to Mer-enjuiti or 1,800 years before Hippocrates according to the European.

You have to understand that the Greek philosophers Pythagoras, Socrates, Plato, Aristotle and even Hippocrates, along with five other Greeks, are the so-called fathers of mathematics, philosophy, technology, science and medicine or in short, academics. This is why in higher mathematics, science and medicine their Greek alphabet is used extensively as variables and their words as terms for definitions. It is also why the college fraternities and sororities use their Greek letters as logos. The funny thing is the European says that during their lifetime, 560

B.C. to 322 B.C., Greece was in an off and on war with the Persians, 540 B.C. to 332 B.C., while at the same time warring with themselves, 431 B.C. to 404 B.C. These wars between Greek city/states were called the Peloponnesian Wars.

This warring between Greek city/states really didn't stop until Alexander the Great put the Greeks under one flag. He declared himself king and acquired full power in 336 B.C. This means that the Peloponnesian Wars actually lasted 95 years. There was only ignorance, chaos, confusion and uncertainty going on in Greece at the time that they were supposed to be the fathers of academia. For any good college student knows it takes peace and quiet to learn anything and the Greeks had no order, peace or discipline at this time.

So, these Greeks had to go elsewhere to learn. Also, at this time, Greek boys began their military training at the age of seven due to their declining male population because of all these wars.

Socrates is revered as being one of these men that began their military training at age seven, trained for about ten years, went to war with the Persians, then turned around and wrote 400 manuscripts. This is impossible. This would mean that Socrates, Plato, Aristotle and Hippocrates would not have had time to learn anything else but military tactics in Greece. Again, they had to have gone elsewhere to have the time to learn something else. It is a fact that this outrageous number of manuscripts is not limited to Socrates it is true for all the Great Greek Philosophers.

This again is impossible due to their short life spans. So, there must be a massive cover up as to the true origin of these manuscripts and thus the origin of the knowledge itself. By the way, the information that these four brought back to Greece was so foreign to them that the Greeks killed Socrates with poison for inseminating this foreign word into the population and then tried to kill Plato with poison also for the same reason. They eventually exiled him into slavery. Aristotle was condemned to death but King Philip of Macedonia put him under his wing saving his life and the knowledge that he possessed.

If this information was theirs to begin with, don't you think the Greeks would be proud of this knowledge and the people who spread it? Now, that number 6,000, for the number of years since the beginning of creation, is starting to look like a secret hand shake isn't it? And those dates made up by the European for the ancient world are there to maintain supremacy. Even the origin of the Masonic Order, with King Solomon and his grandmaster builder, Harim Abif, is only 1,000 B.C. This date is in the time frame where Egypt begins 2,000 years before King Solomon, according to the European.

But according to the Bible, the Pharaoh Shishank, the Libyan King and an invader of the Egyptian throne himself of the 22$^{nd}$ Dynasty, attacked the kingdom of Solomon, I Kings (14:25-26) and II Chronicles (12:1-9), not in 1000 B.C. but a lot closer to 3750 B.C. according to Mer-enjiuti. This is even more of an implication that the original masons were the African Architect Order of the Nile, stretching back to at least 10500 B.C. according to the Pyramid Complex. So, masonry could not have started with Harim Abif.

This date of 3111 B.C. implies that the European had ample time to change the distance of 200 miles that he declared he could see light from the 6$^{th}$ wonder of the world, which was the Lighthouse of Alexandria plus erase its use as a weapon to set ships on fire 35 miles away. Maybe he maintained the distance because its brilliance in light and in accomplishment was so awesome it left a lasting impression on him, especially its ability to burn ships 35 miles away. He needed to remember. This shining example of electricity would remind the European of a better form of artificial light so that he could have a direction to strive towards if he ever became intelligent enough to understand its principles. One more thing, the Lighthouse stood until 1480 A.D. before a series of earthquakes put it into the Mediterranean Sea.

This means that the Lighthouse of Alexandria stood for more than 4,591 years. That's a remarkable feat of engineering. This date also implies that the Africans and the Greeks were married for about 2,300 years before the Romans began to break away from this relationship in 700 B.C. This date of 3111 B.C. further implies that Africa was at peace for all those years. For once again, any successful college student knows it takes peace and quiet to study and learn anything and the Europeans studied hard in Alexandria.

As the critical thinker that I know you are, you also have to remember that the Library of Alexandria housed 1,000,000 manuscripts. So, if it takes peace and quiet to study those manuscripts, what kind of environment had to exist to write those manuscripts—manuscripts dedicated to, but not limited to, mathematics, science, medicine, astronomy, engineering, logic, ethics, metaphysics, technology and philosophy? How much time does it take to write 1,000,000 manuscripts on every subject ever thought of? The answer to the kind of environment and the amount of time required are as follows: Heaven on earth and at least a year for each manuscript. Hopefully the reader will see as I did that there is no other way to accomplish this feat without these conditions being met first. Even if there were only 200,000 manuscripts in the Great Library, as the European declares today, that is still 200,000 years of heaven on earth.

It is the books themselves that justify the existence of the Garden of Eden. You must understand that it was through inquisitive observations and the inevitable recordings of these findings that lead to these manuscripts being placed in the Library of Alexandria in the first place. The European has tried to take credit for what the African has precisely accomplished while he resided in the Garden.

So, how long is this forever that Alexander the Great wanted to inspire? The European says that forever is 298 years. Mer-enjiuti says that forever is at least 3,111 years. In either case they both fall short of Alexander's wishes. It turns out that the people of the earth that know exactly how long forever is, are the Persians (Iranians) for they are the ones that brought the Greeks and the Africans together in the first place. This happened during the second invasion of Africa.

They are the armed forces that Alexander fought against. Ironically, the people that Alexander the Great wanted to bring into the light of humanity and inspire forever eventually did not want his ideal of unity.

*Africa: It's True Role in the Ancient World* •

## Mer-enjuiti a.k.a Menetho and his findings

Europeans say Alexander the Great dies in 323 B.C.
Europeans say Alexandria was completed, Ptolemy I is Pharaoh now 298 B.C.
Europeans ask Professor Mer-enjiuti to write history of Africa 350 B.C.?. Average 323+298+350=971 and 971/3 is 324 but let's round this number to 300 B.C.
Now, Mer-enjiuti says the 1st of the 30 Dynasties began 5,700 years before his time so, 300 + 5,700 equals 6,000
There are at least 6000 years between the 1st of the 30 Dynasties and Jesus's birth

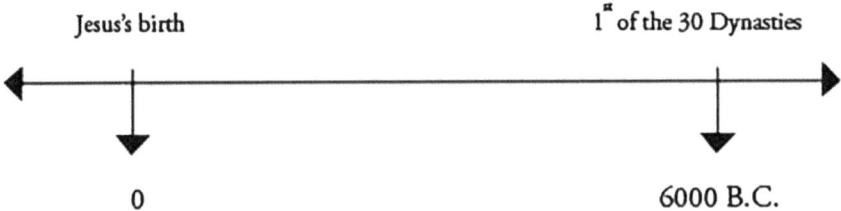

Mer-enjiuti also says that the 30 dynasties lasted for 2,889 years plus the Ptolemaic bloodline mated with the 30th Dynasty. There is no discernable time difference between the completion of Alexandria and the last black dynasty in Egypt.

6,000–2,889 = 3,111 years left over or 3111 B.C. This is when Alexander's Kingdom was completed. This date implies too many things; that is why the European discarded the true time span of Alexander's Kingdom before Jesus Christ.

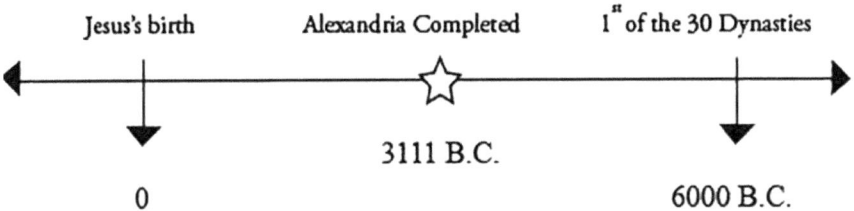

## The Greek Philosophers

The first 5 of the 10 Great Greek Philosophers are:

1. Pythagoras        560 B.C. to 480 B.C. 80 yrs. old
2. Socrates           470 B.C. to 399 B.C. 71 yrs. old
3. Hippocrates      460 B.C. to 377 B.C. 83 yrs. old
4. Plato              427 B.C. to 347 B.C. 80 yrs. old
5. Aristotle          384 B.C. to 322 B.C. 62 yrs. old

Average age of the first five Great European Philosophers = 75.2 years old.

These gentlemen are half of the great Greek philosophers so it can be assumed that they wrote half of the Greek collection of academic writings. That is half of a collection of 2,000 manuscripts. That is 200 manuscripts, on average, for each philosopher. This is impossible considering the fact that during their life times, the Greeks were at war with the Persians, 540 B.C. to 332 B.C. ending with Alexander the Great, and they were at war with themselves, the Peloponnesian war 431 B.C. to 336 B.C. when Alexander put them under one flag. Plus, all the Greek children by age 7 had to study military tactics for at least 10 years to make them fighters because of the decline of the male population due to all the warring. Not to mention that these manuscripts were of mathematics, physics, medicine, engineering, ethics, logic, science, astronomy, music, metaphysics, political science, sociology, teaching and literature. As you can see, the Greeks did not live long enough to learn this material and then write these manuscripts. So, they had to go somewhere else to learn something else.

The only place they could have gone to learn is Egypt. It should be noted that the second 5 of the 10 Great Greek Philosophers all studied in the Kingdom of Alexandria, Egypt.

## SECTION 9

# Carthage: Kingdom of the Moors

Carthage, in North Africa, was in power for 600 years from 800 B.C. to 204 B.C. This kingdom of blacks (because Moor means blacks from North Africa, remember John Hanson and Benjamin Banneker were Moors; moor is the Roman word for black) had a population of 300,000 living in six to ten story apartment buildings (condominiums) and luxurious palaces all constructed with the finest marble. This kingdom had hot and cold running water, heating and air conditioning, showers and flushing toilets, fountains and hanging gardens. Every citizen of Carthage had access to its utilities for free years before Rome had utilities of any sort.

Unlike the Romans, who eventually ran their water in aqueducts above ground, the Carthaginians ran their water underground downhill from the mountains to pressurize their plumbing system. This system was also supplied with collected rainwater in the buildings filtered reservoirs. The European will tell you some trumped up fable about Carthage originating with a woman running from the city of Tyre located on the north eastern side of the Mediterranean Sea to escape her brother's wrath after he killed her husband or something or other. The truth is Carthage was founded by students from the University of Alexandria as a classroom assignment handed out by the professors and master teachers of that institution just like Greece before them and Rome soon after.

The Carthaginian Hanno the Navigator, in 520 B.C., is accredited with sailing to expand the boundaries of Carthage. The islands of Sardinia, Corsica and Balearic became properties of the kingdom under his rule. Hanno is also accredited with sailing through the pillars of Hercules to the Americas 1,992 years before Columbus. For 200 years, Carthage dominated the Mediterranean Sea until the coming of Rome. Carthage and Rome soon found themselves in conflict over the pearl of the Mediterranean Sea, the island of Sicily.

Sicily was an important piece of property in the middle of the vital trade routes of the Mediterranean and whoever controlled Sicily controlled the trade routes and controlled the wealth. The Romans began to establish themselves on the island and the Carthaginians told them that they were there first and to please leave. But, the eastern side of Sicily sided with Rome. This caused great tension between the two nations and it would lead to war. These wars would be known as the Punic Wars. In the 3rd century B.C., the Republic of Rome, as it was called before Caesar Augustus, would be committing piracies against Carthage on land and in the sea. This angered the Carthaginians and thus began the first Punic War. Punic War I started in 264 B.C. Seventeen years later, Rome and Carthage were still deadlocked in a bloody battle until one of the greatest military geniuses of all time took control of Carthage. His name is Hamilcar Barca. Hamilcar lived from 270 B.C. to 228 B.C. When he was about 23 years old, **he swept his army into Sicily like a storm front, changing the outcome of the war in the favor of Carthage.** Hamilcar also bought war ships from Greece, making their Tryrins into Quinqerins. This effectively made the Greek ships bigger and faster to defeat the Romans ships at sea. The Carthaginians won many battles at sea against the Romans. So, the Romans also bought ships from the Greeks in secret and made them into ships like the Carthaginians as best they could. The Greeks were in it for the money not knowing that 92 years later they would pay for that deal with Rome with the sovereignty of their nation after the battle of Corinth. Their lives were also the price with the quelling of the Spartacus Rebellion 70 years after that.

The Carthaginian and Roman navies met at the Aegates Islands off the northern coast of Sicily. The European would have you believe that the impending military campaign was a face-to-face, fair and honorable naval battle, it wasn't. Carthage had already defeated the Romans, ending Punic War I. So, they began establishing their supply lines shipping food and supplies to their camps in Sicily and beyond. The Carthaginians did not know the Greeks sold them out to the Romans. The Carthaginian navy was a sitting duck bulging with supplies like fat cows when the Romans ambushed them in ships like their own. The Carthaginians lost to the Romans who were in ships that were so poorly designed, so poorly engineered that the Roman ships used that day fell apart a year later.

They sure served their purpose though. Rome now owned the western half of the Mediterranean Sea. The Romans captured nearly 30,000 Carthaginian soldiers, now slaves, and Hamilcar was forced to retreat to Carthage. In victory, the Romans gained the islands of Sicily, Sardinia, Corsica and Balearic and then forced Carthage to pay a large tribute to Rome to cripple Carthage even further.

**Hamilcar never forgot the ambush from Rome and the betrayal of Greece after winning Punic war I.** So, he decided to launch a sneak attack of his own. He convinced the elders of Carthage of his plans and they agreed, sending him to Spain in 237 B.C. to carry them out.

First, he began by defeating the Barbarians in Spain and plundering their land to spread the might of Carthage. He fought for nine years conquering the land and finally making Spain a Carthaginian territory. He paid for this victory with his life in 228 B.C. Hamilcar's son, ***Hannibal Barca***, took over at this time.

Born in 247 B.C. Hannibal made a promise to his father when he was nine years old. His father declared that he would take his son with him on his conquest of Spain but only if Hannibal promised to hate the Romans and continue the plan to destroy them if necessary. (Notice that if Hamilcar lost at sea through negligence by his own accord as history teaches, then why did the elders of Carthage entrust the sanctity and sovereignty of their land to this careless leader?)

Hamilcar taught his son everything he knew about the Romans while in Spain and instilled in him the hatred of their enemy. After his father's death, Hannibal Barca had use of the world's greatest engineering core and in 221 B.C., Punic War II started. Hannibal took command of the Carthaginian Army and launched the most stunning sneak attack the world has ever seen.

Rome had control over the western half of the Mediterranean Sea, which meant that Hannibal couldn't attack Rome that way. Driven to fulfill the promise he made to his father, Hannibal set out to do the impossible, the unthinkable. He would march over land to get to the heart of Rome. Hannibal would take an army of 90,000 troops, 12,000 horses and 37 African elephants across 3 raging rivers, the Loire, the Rhone and the Po plus through 5 mountain ranges, the Pyrenees, the Massif Central, the Jura, the Alps, and the Apennines to fight the Romans on their own ground. Yes, I said through the mountains not over them like that army in the movie "Return of the King".

This course of action that Hannibal took should remind you of a great Motown classic containing the lyrics "Ain't no mountain high enough, ain't no river wide enough, ain't no valley low enough to keep me from getting to you". These lyrics speak of the power of love, Hence, logically, hatred or loathing must be the opposite of love, not indifference as the dictionary declares because it is just as powerful if not more and Hannibal surely did not love his enemy. No one would expect such an action to be possible even in the modern world. He was definitely motivated. The question is what kind of engineering skills did the ancients possess that we today have forgotten?

Five years later in 216 B.C., Hannibal could see the northern plains of Italy and he knew Rome was not prepared for his sneak attack. Carthage makes a stand against Rome on Roman soil and wins. Hannibal's army killed 70,000 Roman soldiers and 10,000 of them were taken as prisoners, it was a good day. However, Hannibal was unable to capitalize on his victories. He fought for another 13 years but was never able to capture Rome. If any one of those three ranging rivers or five mountain ranges were not there in his way then

Rome would surely have been destroyed. Hannibal was so terrifying, so dreadful to the Romans during his time in Italy that his name still evokes a notion of fear in the European even today, hence the character Hannibal Lector.

Ironically, during this time period, 214 B.C., the Greek Mathematician Archimedes was saving the city of Syracuse located on the eastern shore of Sicily from the tyranny of Rome. He had the Greek soldiers polish their brass shields and then focus them in unison at the attacking Roman Navy. The Roman ships were set ablaze in the sea. This simple demonstration of the focused power of the sun has been known as the Archimedes Death Ray.

The Romans later killed Archimedes in 212 B.C. and the Greeks were kicked out of Sicily. The eastern Sicilians certainly had a change of heart all of a sudden with respect to the Romans, didn't they? The Romans wanted Archimedes' scientific mind for military gain. They sent a few soldiers to collect him in Sicily. But when Archimedes did not leave with them because of the importance of his research, one of the soldiers became infuriated enough to kill the insolent academic. You have to know that this particular soldier was executed in the worst way by the republic. His suffering had to be legendary.

In 204 B.C., Rome went on the offensive and launched an assault on the Kingdom of Carthage. Hannibal returned home to defend his kingdom. In 202 B.C., Hannibal was defeated at the battle of Zama and then forced to surrender to an enemy he had spent his whole life trying to destroy. Hannibal was respected by the Romans so much for his daring attempts to destroy them that they exiled him to Turkey where in 183 B.C. he committed suicide. Carthage was forced to pay high taxes to Rome and give up their territories and their military might. The Carthaginians could no longer take up arms without Rome's approval.

The Romans were now poised to take over the world. The Romans knew that Carthage was too close to them to be trusted to be allowed to exist. The Roman orator Kato wanted Carthage destroyed and he ended every speech with "Carthage must be destroyed". At this time, its southern neighbor, Numidia, was bullying Carthage. So, Carthage took up arms to defend herself.

This was in direct violation of the treaty written after Punic War II. Rome finds out about this and claims that Carthage will be after them next. "Carthage must be destroyed." Rome tells Carthage that they must evacuate the kingdom. Carthage refuses to do so and this starts Punic War III which lasts about three years. In 152 B.C., Rome sent an overwhelming army to Carthage to destroy it. The Carthaginian General, Hasdrubal, prepares his people for war. The Carthaginian walls held the Romans at bay for three years. The Romans were able to breach the walls at sea then set the kingdom on fire for fear of sniper attacks. In 149 B.C., Carthage was destroyed. Rome would later rebuild the city because of its strategic location.

Note, that same year scholars say that Rome conquered Greece at the battle of Corinth and 70 years later quelled the Spartacus Rebellion, making the Greeks the first people to be crucified on a massive scale by the Romans. During this time period Paul wrote two thirds of the New Testament. The Romans perfected the art of crucifixion on 6,000 Greek soldiers while putting them all on public display along the entire span of a road named the Appian Way. This road ran between the cities of Capua and Rome, a distance of 270 miles. I would say that the Greeks made a fatal error in choosing the Romans over the Carthaginians, wouldn't you?

*Africa: It's True Role in the Ancient World* •

## The Kingdom of Carthage 650 B.C.

## The Kingdom of Carthage, Hanno the Navigator 550 B.C.

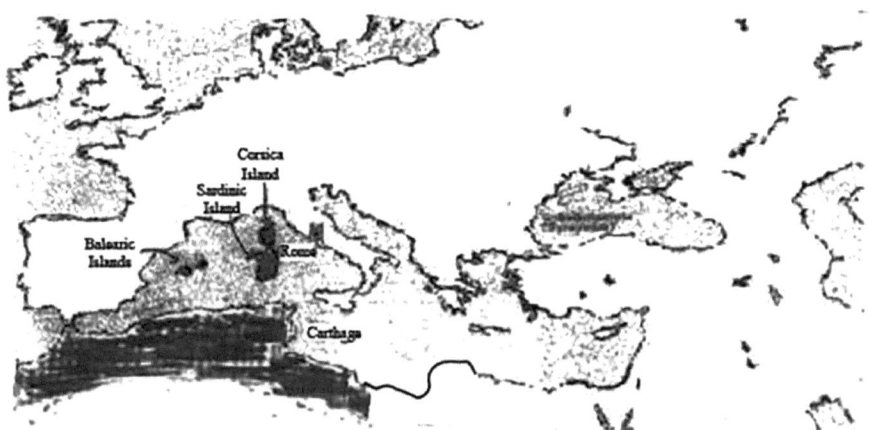

The Kingdom of Carthage and the Republic of Rome
Battle over Sicily 285 B.C.
Punic War I Starts 264 B.C.
Hamilcar Barca

Hamilcar Barca captures Spain, in 228 B.C.
Hannibal Barca takes over at this time

*Africa: It's True Role in the Ancient World* •

In 221 B.C. Punic War II Starts
Hannibal Barca marches to Rome

Hannibal Barca is defeated in 202 B.C. at the battle
of Zama Hasdrubal Starts Punic III in 152 B.C.

Scholars say Greece is defeated by the Republic of Rome that same year, 149 B.C.
The Territory of the Republic of Rome after Punic War III

By 133 B.C. Rome had conquered Carthage and Greece but clearly they did not have Egypt or Alexander's Kingdom

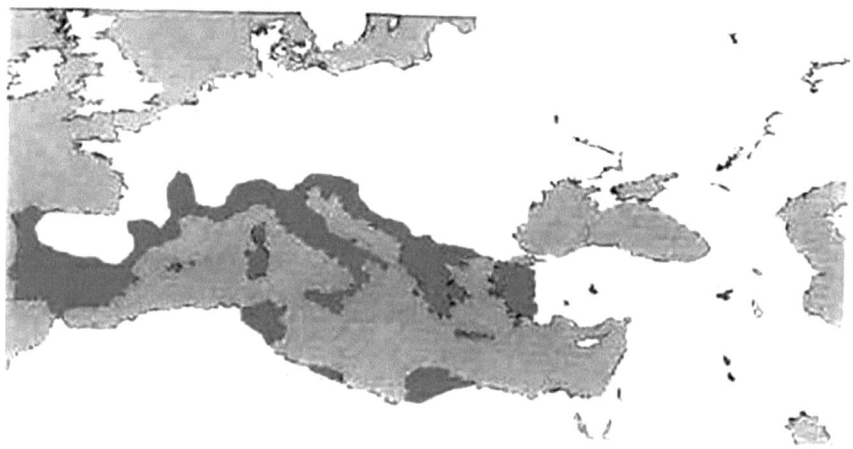

# SECTION 10

# Rome, the Conjecture

After thinking critically about this for the past thirty years, I have come to the realization that the Romans came into existence out of hatred, a hatred for the African who was assimilating the Greeks into blackness, a blackness that is the natural state of man. The Romans held a hatred for the African despite the knowledge and old-world manners that they were receiving from him. The Romans wanted to stay white and rule Africa like the Tamahu, Hyksos and Troglodytes before them. Moreover, the Romans were the embodiment of the last of the blonde haired, blue-eyed Europeans.

To switch gears for a moment, there was a modern-day experiment done on lions in the African jungle broadcasted on the Discover Channel in the 1990's. Two stuffed male lion dummies were covered in the same male lion urine and placed in a grassy area of the jungle. One of the lions had a blonde mane and the other had a black mane. After a while, several female lions in a group walked up, smelled and rubbed up against both male lion dummies. Eventually, in a very short period of time, all of the female lions preferred the lion with the black mane and they preferred him as a group completely rejecting the lion with the blonde mane.

Now, applying this information to the Romans, no woman would mate with this blonde-haired blue-eyed man given a choice between him and the African. The African had everything a man could want at that time. The Roman women didn't even want the Roman men. The Roman fraternity on the campus of Alexandria resorted to homosexuality to compensate for this dilemma.

Concurrent with this problem, the blonde haired blue-eyed European could not activate his pineal gland. The pineal gland is a single gland at the roof of the third ventricle in the middle of the two hemispheres of the brain at the apex of the spinal cord located at the geometric center of the brain case like the Great Pyramid is located in the geographical center of all of the landmasses. The pineal gland is also present in all vertebrates. The Indians from India wear a dot on their forehead to represent this gland and its potential. In 1776 A.D., a branch of the Masonic Order, called the Illuminati, developed a chart that explains the purpose of this gland and others in the body. The Ancient Greeks called the pineal gland the "Third Eye", the seat of the soul. This gland is also mentioned in the Holy Bible as a way to meet God face-to-face (Genesis 32:30-31).

Today, however, the Europeans say its function is obscure but in truth it is the activation of this gland that allows a stable connection with the architect of the universe, a connection with God as he said as an Ancient Greek. Funny, in 2,000 years, the European made a complete turnaround on the issue, didn't he? To open the eye took 40 years of intense study in Egypt where it was perfected over countless eons.

This discipline was made available to the European at the University of Alexandria where he was a student. This gland is activated after the student has mastered self, controlling one's emotions and thoughts so the eye could be opened through concentration and relaxation. The problem for the blonde-haired blue-eyed Europeans is that the pineal gland is melanin motivated and melanin activated.

It is the melanin factor that is required before the gland can be accessed despite the forty years of study. Imagine going to school for 39 years, sacrificing, preparing for all that time learning the discipline, controlling and mastering self so that you can receive the nexus of the pineal gland and only then finding out in your 40th year of study that you can't activate it because you are melanin deficient and therefore inferior. In short, the European could not see beyond his five senses because he could not activate his pineal gland.

These events of female rejection and non-connection to the source of all things told the European that he is inferior. And instead of bowing out gracefully and allowing his condition to be swallowed up by the dominant gene, he went insane and began planning to close the 3$^{rd}$ eye in everyone else. This is a classic case of "If I can't use my pineal gland then neither will anyone else." In other words, the European reacted like a child.

These two events fueled their anger and they became a rogue fraternity. This fraternal order became a new occult of the followers of Seth, they became Romans. Now in their fifties, this fraternity banded together under a new order, a new philosophy. This philosophy was of white power, Arian Brotherhood and world domination set down in the year 700 B.C. To grow their population, the Romans had to brainwash and rape the white female to bring her into the group in order to create more followers. The Roman fraternity grew in secret and established a colony in Italy called Rome. It was their "Animal House". It is here that the Romans made enemies of Carthage, an enemy that almost destroyed them. This 115-year war with Carthage drove Rome over the edge. The Romans went north first after defeating Carthage then defeated the armies of Spartacus, making Greece and its territories Roman property in 79 B.C. Most scholars say Rome conquered Greece as early as 149 B.C. with the battle of Corinth. That was right after Carthage. Most importantly the Romans continued north conquering most of present day France in 58 B.C. Around 54 B.C., the Romans came back south to Alexandria, Egypt. These historic events imply that the Romans waited until the last male pharaoh died leaving the kingdom to a woman before they betrayed Egypt, diplomatically. (Remember, the Europeans declared the city of Rome was established in 700 B.C. and Cleopatra VII, daughter of Ptolemy XII, the last pharaoh of Africa to rule Alexandria, the capital of the Mediterranean world, was forced to commit suicide by the Romans around 34 B.C. The significance of these two dates will be revealed later).

Forty-five-year-old Julius Caesar was sent to Egypt by the Roman Senate to present their list of proposals, i.e. demands to the Royal

Court. Nineteen-year-old Queen Cleopatra used the only bargaining chips she had, her intellect and her female charm. She was also fluent in nine languages. To get his attention she unrolled herself out of a red carpet and presented herself to Caesar in fishnets. This theatrical and dramatic event with the red carpet is so ingrained in the European's subconscious mind that it has been used as a staple at all of his high-profile events ever since.

Meanwhile, she took him on the same tour of Egypt that Alexander the Great went on at least 3,100 years earlier. The only difference came when Julius Caesar was taken to the museum that housed Alexander's mummified body as its centerpiece. This mummy was the proof to the legacy of her nation's greatness, longevity and their people's shared past. Julius Caesar fell in love with Cleopatra and her way because it was the right way of life as Alexander concluded at least 3,100 years earlier. He did not want to take over Egypt any more. They later had a son named Caesarian who was to be the unifier of Egypt and Rome. The child was supposed to establish a new covenant between Africa and Europe, renewing the commitment of Alexander the Great.

This infuriated the Roman Senate and they killed Julius on "The Ides of March", March 14th 44 B.C. with their own hands and then sent Mark Anthony to finish the job that Julius obviously could not accomplish. It should be noted that not only did Julius Caesar prevent the Roman Republic from falling apart due to civil strife; he also doubled the size of the Roman territories. This is a man Rome should have revered and celebrated, not executed. This is the real reason for his murder.

Cleopatra took Mark Anthony on the same tour that Julius Caesar went on and Mark Anthony became a traitor to the Roman order, falling in love with her and her way for the same reasons. Cleopatra gave birth to his twins and a third child. Meanwhile, Caesarian, the unifier, was 10 years old. Furthermore, when Mark Anthony was unsuccessful in carrying out his duties, together with subsidizing Roman territories to his new lover, the Senate of Rome launched a war campaign against Egypt. Mark Anthony used his fleet of ships to defend his lover and her way. Octavian, adopted son of Julius Caesar, lead this war campaign, which took seven years to accomplish. Altogether it took 19 years, from Julius Caesar's tour of Egypt to Queen Cleopatra's forced suicide, for Rome to take Egypt over militarily once the Romans decided to betray their master teachers.

To commemorate this momentous victory, the Romans changed Octavius' name to Augustus and declared him Caesar. They executed Caesarian and then changed the Egyptian week from ten days to seven, this is why the week is seven days today. When Cleopatra was dead, the Romans gained the Kingdom of Alexandria and then moved Alexander's mummified body against his will to Rome. Rome was now the capital of The Mediterranean World. The Romans also gained the 1,293,768 square miles of fertile Nile Valley to feed their hungry army. The Roman Republic was now the Roman Empire. It turns out that the life of Caesarian justifies the true length of this uneasy time period between Egypt and Rome for he lived through it all save perhaps 2 years. He lived to be 17 years old and was executed right after his mother-committed suicide.

Now, if Alexander the Great conquered Egypt, as the Europeans say he did, then it should have been a Greek territory and Rome should have acquired this territory immediately after the defeat of Greece, either in 79 B.C. or even as early as 149 B.C. with the battle of Corinth when many scholars say Greece was conquered by Rome. They clearly did not acquire Egypt then or Augustus would not be known as the Roman Emperor to conquer Egypt plus Rome would not have had to go through all that drama with Cleopatra. This also implies that Egypt was always a sovereign nation until Cleopatra's forced suicide in 34 B.C. This means that Alexander was a liberator and patriot of Africa against a common Persian enemy and not a conqueror of Africa as has been accepted.

No Greek moved Alexander's mummified body to Greece in protest to its display on foreign soil. There it remained in Egypt for at least 3,111 years until Rome violated his orders.

Now, if you take 34 from 700 you get a number that looks a lot like 666. The true meaning of this number is that it took the Romans

666 years from the inception of their philosophy to total domination over Egypt, which was actually the real WWI. Remember, the same region of the world the Romans occupied until they took their so-called last stand in 530 A.D. started the two wars that were fought in 1914 A.D. and 1939 A.D. Moreover, these two wars were fought under the same philosophy and principles the Romans stood for and the same philosophy and principles that Hitler declared that his Germans should live up to, to become their ancestors.

Also, the Nazi forces called WWII the Third Reich, not the Second. The Germans say the First Reich was the Holy Roman Empire in which they say began in 800 A.D. and lasted until 1806 A.D. The truth is the First Reich is when the Romans conquered Egypt, their host and master teachers, becoming an empire in 34 B.C. not before. Nevertheless, if you want to know what the Romans looked like and the demeanor of a Roman just watch some old Hitler films and you'll see what Jesus had to put up with.

Notice that since Cleopatra's forced suicide, the African has not ruled at his capacity. This is completely by design and made possible by the Roman motivation to stay white and rule at any cost. The Romans also murdered Jesus and after finding out that he was God, they still attacked the people of Jerusalem and Judah, then hunted down the 900 people of Masada that followed his example 73 years after his murder. The 900 rebels fled the Roman's tyranny in Judah to King Herod's abandoned palace on top of a 1,500-foot tall, 900-foot long, 300-foot wide plateau called Masada, a mountain stronghold in the middle of the Judean desert near the Dead Sea.

Then after a two-year long siege on these people that had done no wrong, the Romans finally forced the peaceful people of Masada to commit suicide by bringing their siege machines along with legions of soldiers up a man-made ramp built to run to the top of the mountain. Suicide to the people of Masada was a better alternative than being raped and tortured to death by their enemy. Essentially, they robbed the Romans of their victory by taking away the spoils of victory, robbing them of their pride and morale. Think about it, the Romans after two long years of dreaming of finishing off these rebels and making this incident an example of Roman dominance the Romans find dead bodies and eerie silence upon reaching the top of the mountain. After which, in 76 A.D., the Romans, under Emperor Vespasian, who was the general over the Masada incident, built the Coliseum with slave labor to stop all rebellions started by the Cleo wars, Jesus Christ and the Masada incident. In addition, Rome was attempting to regain their lost pride and morale. By the way, this should not be a surprise the Romans built all of their cities with slave labor not just the Coliseum. One in three citizens of the Roman Empire was a slave.

This structure, called the Apocalypse by the Roman lower class, was designed to exterminate the knowledge base in Africa because the horrific torture device known as "The Cross" was not working as a single deterrent to rebellions against the Roman order. But do not be fooled this device was not abandoned at all it was still used in the Coliseum games for theatrical purposes. This structure of doom is the reason why Africans do not remember who they are or what they have accomplished. The Coliseum stood for 400 years from 79 A.D. to 479 A.D. I have calculated that if 100 Africans were killed within the bowels of this structure each day, 300 days a year for 400 years that is a minimum of 12,000,000 African rebels dead and can no longer teach the people the truth about themselves, the Romans or the past.

Ironically, the source of the rebellions, the University/Kingdom of Alexandria, was allowed to remain open, from Queen Cleopatra's suicide and Jesus' murder all the way to 415 A.D. when the Roman Emperor Theodosius II ordered its destruction. This means that the Library and the Coliseum coexisted for 339 years. The Romans allowed the University to remain open until they felt they did not need this miracle anymore. In 415 A.D., the Romans burned the University of Alexandria down along with about 700,000 manuscripts, including most of the volumes of Mer- enjiuti in the Great Library. The Coliseum lasted for another 61 years before Rome lost 95% of its population due to ignorance. They finally fell into darkness around 530 A.D.

Within that period from the year 320 A.D. to 500 A.D., the European did all he could to cover up his crime, his original sin. Emperor Constantine the Great moved the capital of Rome to present day Istanbul, their insurance policy and new base of operations in the year 324 A.D. He made this move just in case the Roman Empire collapsed. Constantine was just being prudent. He was aware of the previous emperors overspending and their fleecing of the territories and reasoned that their indulgences may have irreversibly damaged the empire. He was right.

This new capital was strategically located on both sides of the Bosporus, which again is a body of water that connects the Black Sea with the Aegean Sea and separates Europe from Asia. The Romans spent the next 120 years setting up shop here. They moved all of their spoils of Rome to the new capital, which was completed in 355 A.D. and then named it after its founder. Meanwhile, Rome was being sacked constantly. Later, the Romans built a wall around the new capital to keep the enemies of Rome out. The wall was completed in 450 A.D. just in time to stop Attila the Hun.

After Rome fell in 530 A.D., Constantinople then became the capital of the Byzantine Empire, Eastern Rome, lasting for 1,100 years. Constantinople, over time, became the richest city in the world. It had hot and cold running water, heating, air conditioning, showers, flushing toilets, fountains and hanging gardens. (The European did not become a Christian until Emperor Constantine accepted it as a religion and the people did not accept it completely until 400 A.D. The cross and the sword were the implements used to motivate the Romans in this direction. The implication is that all Christians that the Romans were persecuting before they accepted it as a religion were not European… I wonder who they were?)

There were two major conferences that were organized to meet several objectives to maintain European dominance for the purpose of political and social control plus to distort the African truth. This was due to the fact that the Romans were losing power militarily. These are the two conferences that did the most damage. These conferences are known as the conference of Nicaea in 325 A.D. and the conference of Ephesus in 431 A.D. where Emperor Theodosius II de-Africanized the Holy Royal Family of Isis, Heru and Osiris.

In 325 A.D. Emperor Constantine summoned all the Bishops of Rome living around the Mediterranean Sea to a conference at his palace in Nicean to determine what doctrines would be incorporated into their Christian religion. During this conference, the European put the 66 books of the Bible together in his favor including the one he named "Romans" so that the common man would not question Roman benevolence while discarding at least 47 books that did not suit their motives, these books are known as "The lost books of the Bible". Then they wrote the African saints out of religion and very few Africans complained about this or anything else the Romans corrupted because they killed the lot of them in the Coliseum for a period of 245 years up to this point. So, how can we expect to be getting the truth in the Christian faith when you become aware of what the Romans did to that faith?

The Romans renamed the Holy Royal Trinity of Africa that consisted of Isis, Heru and Osiris to Mary and Jesus respectively then dropped Joseph. The Romans then painted them white in 431 A.D. at the conference of Ephesus. Now, back in 325 A.D., scholars say that Constantine saw the cross in a vision while he was on the battlefield and declared, "In this symbol we shall conquer". Scholars also say Constantine took the looped cross, the Ankh, reduced the size of the loop then closed it to form the cross that we worship today. Later, the Romans put Jesus on it figuratively this time to make this the new symbol of Christianity, replacing the fish of old. Today, it has been proven that the cross is the Egyptian symbol for peace that Constantine actually found while he was in Egypt closing the temples and schools to effectively close the minds of the conquered people that remained. In this same time period John Paul convinced the Visigoths to spare Rome after beating the Romans senseless.

When John Paul saved Rome by negotiating a yearly pay-off of protection money so that they could complete this mission of corruption, Europe made him the first Pope. They made him the top of the Christian hierarchy by putting a double crown of lower Africa on his head and an African nailed to two sticks as a scepter. These symbols for the leader of their most secret society are more than appropriate. The crown of lower Africa is used because lower Africa is North Africa and Europe is north of the Nile Delta and north of the Mediterranean Sea, hence the double crown. An African nailed to two sticks is used as a scepter because that is what they had to do to gain power and assume the African legacy.

They had to exterminate and the main device used for this mass extermination was the torture device known as "The Cross". This is sick if you think about it too much but it is the truth and as the elders say, the truth will set you free.

The European then created heaven and hell to further strengthen their control over the people and then made up the ten percent rule to make money off of those they controlled through fear. During this time, the Romans took off their suits of armor and put on the robes of the Priest, Bishop, Archbishop and the Pope as cover while the rest of Western Rome collapses around them.

Then the Europeans, as Byzantines, under Emperor Theodosius II and then Justinian I, sent a highly educated elite squad of green-beret soldiers back into Africa to close the rest of the schools and temples as well as destroy everything that made the African appear to be superior to them, everything that made the African look as though he was ever enfolded in lady knowledge, everything that made the African stand out as a true man of God and everything that made the African a role model.

**The European even** distorted the timeline to hide his educational dependency to the African and to hide the African's true contribution to society. The Europeans did this cover-up for one reason and one reason only; they knew they had 2,000 overdue manuscripts from the Library of Alexandria in their possession stored behind the walls of Constantinople. After the burning of the University of Alexandria was completed, the new knowledge base would now be in Europe. Sooner or later, the European knew he would wake up to the knowledge of Alexandria and its modern tendencies before the African would. Until then, the European could always hold the African in contempt mentally, physically and spiritually by deceiving, then later forcing the African to build kingdoms for him until the time the European could open his eyes and become a thinker again.

This dark period in Western Europe lasted for 780 years from 530 A.D. to 1310 A.D., after which the crusades of the Knights Templar netted African manuscripts, originally from the Library of Alexandria, from the Islamic Empire located on the east coast of the Mediterranean Sea. The question is how did Western Europeans translate Arabic into something he could read without the help of the Arab? Answer, the European found his help in Spain, located on the western side of the Mediterranean Sea. It was also a part of the Islamic Empire.

The Western European went to school at the Universities of Salamanca and Granada in Spain and the University of Timbuktu in West Africa for 350 years from 1100 A.D. to 1450 A.D. trading and studying with people of color for the second time.

Scholars also say that the Knights Templar acquired the treasure of King Solomon's mines at this time and used it to pay the Masons to build the castles, temples, cathedrals and universities of Europe during the middle ages.

The Pope was upset by the weird rituals the Templar's had acquired while fighting in the Holy Land. He called it heresy and began hunting them down and torturing them to death. The survivors hid under the cloak of the Masonic Order where their rituals became one. It should be noted that the Pope is the one who sent the Knights Templar to the so- called Holy Land in 1099 A.D. to liberate it from the infidels of Islam as history teaches. Yet, they left the region as soon as they found the books of antiquity and never went back. The Islamic Empire is still there today. So why were the Knights Templar really there?

After 210 years of loyal service, blood, sweat and tears fighting in the Holy Land for the Pope, the Pope then betrayed his holy warriors even after they helped remove the veil of darkness, finally bringing Western Europe into the light of comprehension again.

So, who were these Knights Templars, these holy warriors anyway? What kind of people made up their ranks? If we remove the mystique surrounding them, we find an army composed of medieval knights (thugs) and ex-Vikings (gangsters). These were trained killers from the past wars between the Vikings and Europe that now found it difficult to hang up their swords even after a decree of peace was reached. To stop them from fighting among themselves, the church unified them, paid them well, and gave them a purpose. The church led the Templars into Islam to take the knowledge.

Before 1310 A.D., the Western European suffered through plagues, diseases, pestilence, ignorance and the constant threat of war while in Eastern Europe, the Byzantine Empire was a beacon of light, holding the knowledge and the truth about Africa and Europe behind walls for 1,100 years. The walls of Byzantium finally fell victim to the gun powdered powered cannon by the hands of a group of Muslims called the Ottomans in 1453 A.D. The capital city of Constantine now would be forever known as Istanbul. Inevitably, its 2,000 manuscripts from antiquity would be available to the west, igniting the European Renaissance period. Soon after this, the European built three empires on Africa's back that at one time for each empire the sun never set. These empires included France, England and Spain, after which the European started working on the Americas, then his enlightenment period started.

It should also be noted that the bloodline of the Roman Senate is still alive and fully functional today as the upper echelon of the Roman Catholic Church and other prestigious secret orders. As Roman Catholics, this bloodline sanctioned the Holy Inquisition, the Crusades, African slavery, and the Spanish and Enlightenment Inquisitions making this organization responsible for over 175,000,000 murders, $6/7^{th}$ of which were non-European.

Unfortunately, these murders do not include the millions of African rebels murdered by the laws of the Roman Senate during their conquest of the Mediterranean World and inevitable established order of the Roman Empire.

The Roman Catholics, as we know them today, have been around for 1,500 years and counting. For those that question these facts, they only need to take note of the English alphabet and the modern western calendar. This alphabet is saturated with 88.5% of the Roman alphabet and the western calendar, the Gregorian calendar, literally has three months named after two Caesars of Rome, July for Julius Caesar, August for Augustus Caesar and October for Augustus' given name, Octavian. This is not a coincidence.

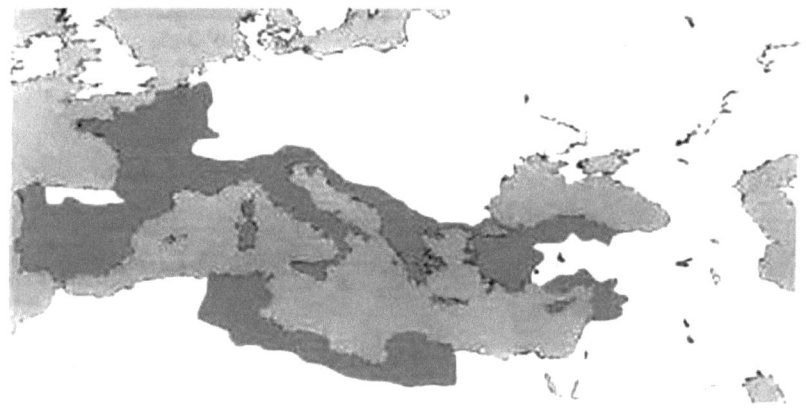

40 B.C. Caesar

Even by 40 B.C. after Julius' murder, clearly they still did not have Egypt or Alexander's Kingdom. (They used 30 B.C. to hide the truth about the relationship between the birth of the Roman Republic, 700 B.C., and the real year of the death of Queen Cleopatra, 34 B.C., 700- 34= 666). The Roman didn't acquire Egypt until after Queen Cleopatra's death, becoming an empire only then and not before.

79 A.D.: Vespasian

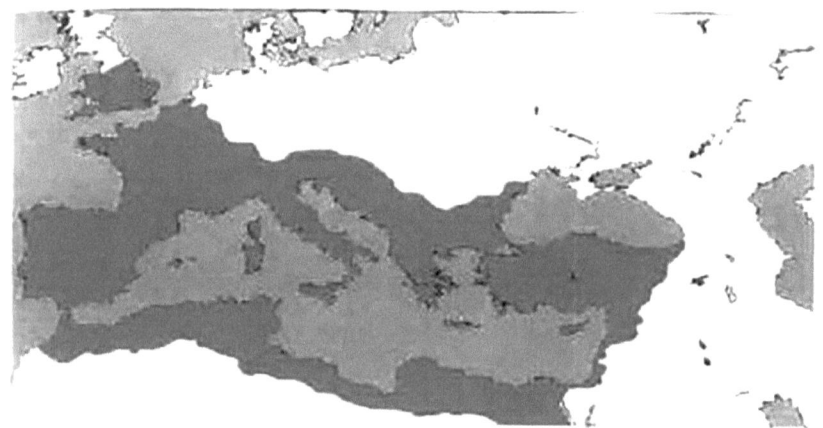

The Roman Empire

Vespasian built the Coliseum to kill all rebels and maintain Roman Order and morale.

*Africa: It's True Role in the Ancient World* •

## 330 A.D.: A New Empire

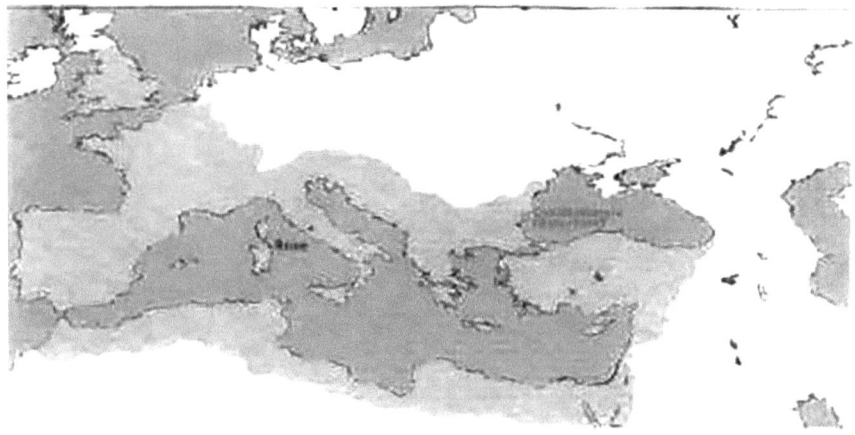

## The Roman Empire

Constantine just finished mapping out his new base of operations just in case the total Empire of Rome could not be maintained.

Pope John Paul II

The Crown of Lower Egypt (left) and the Crown of Upper Egypt (right)

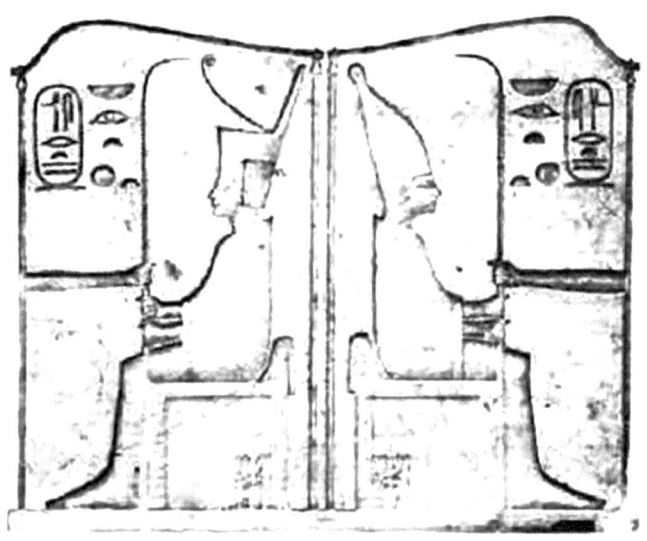

# SECTION 11

# My Thoughts

In 574 B.C., the Babylonians/Persians defeated the so-called origin of Carthage, the city of Tyre on the northeast bank of the Mediterranean Sea, in present day Turkey. Why didn't the Carthaginians help their brothers in Tyre? The Persians also fought the Greeks in an off and on war from 540 B.C. to 332 B.C., finally being defeated by a Greek named Alexander the Great whose kingdom in northeast Africa was completed in 298 B.C. according to the European. Greece is a lot closer to the city of Rome than Rome is to Carthage, which is in North Africa. So, why did the Romans decide to interact with Carthage instead of Greece?

The Romans could have helped the Greeks in their Persian War. We should all know how much the Romans like to fight, praying for war when there wasn't one. So why didn't they? Let's look at the events again. The first war between Carthage and Rome was called Punic War I. It was fought on land and in the Mediterranean Sea from 264 B.C. to 241 B.C. Carthage had redesigned Greek ships and won Punic War I. Then later, with regard to Greek ships, so did the Romans, as stated by the European. The Romans won because they ambushed the Carthaginian ships while they were full of supplies, to Carthage, who was busy expanding their economy, the war was already won. The point here is both had contact with the Greeks and both could have helped them in their Persian War at least 200 years earlier because Carthage and Rome originated in the year 800 B.C. and 700 B.C. respectively. And again, for the Romans, there was a war going on in their own backyard and they chose not to help and not to fight. Why?

In 214 B.C., the Romans turned their attention on Greece now that they were rulers of the sea. Archimedes saved the Greeks on the eastern shores of Sicily with his death ray of polished brass shields. He had the Greek army train the sun's light energy on the Roman ships to set them on fire in the sea, keeping them at bay for 65 to 135 years depending on who you listen to. Now, the second Punic War between Carthage and Rome was fought on land from 221 B.C. to 202 B.C. Carthage crossed five mountain ranges and three raging rivers to destroy Rome for their cowardice ambush. The Romans won this one because Carthage ran out of supplies this time. In 202 B.C., Rome gave Carthage their list of demands. The Romans later launched a third Punic War to completely destroy Carthage after a 50-year campaign strategy called "Carthage Must Be Destroyed". In 149 B.C. Rome destroyed Carthage and took over Greece that same year. Now the Romans were truly ready to take over the rest of the Mediterranean World as stated by the European.

Ok, after their cowardice conquering of Carthage, the Romans waited another 70 years at most to take over Greece, again, depending on which scholar you listen to, then in 58 B.C. Julius Caesar took four legions of Roman soldiers and conquered Gaul, present day France, in essences they waited another 25 years after the conquest of Greece to bring their list of proposals i.e. demands back across the Mediterranean Sea to Queen Cleopatra, Queen of the Kingdom of Alexandria, in the year 53 B.C. This kingdom was only 245 years old at that time according to the European. A kingdom that was 291 years younger than Carthage was during the first Punic War. If you think about it, why didn't Rome, back in 149 B.C. just continue from Carthage east along the coast of Africa, either by land or by sea, and take over this 149-year-old kingdom? This 149-year-old kingdom was at this time 387 years younger than Carthage was during the first Punic War. The Romans had the manpower and supplies to do it too. Why did the

Romans decide to go back north, defeat Greece first and present-day France, then bring this list of demands to the Kingdom of Alexandria in Africa? Then waste precious time bowing on one knee to a woman for 12 years before they decided to go to war with her for another 7?

They could have avoided Cleopatra altogether while they were already on the African continent and marched into Alexandria and took it over a full 76 years before she was ever born. Why did Rome hesitate? As previously mentioned, if Alexander conquered Egypt then Rome should have acquired Egypt immediately after conquering Greece in 79 B.C. (Scholars say Greece was defeated by Rome in 149 B.C. right after Carthage at the battle of Corinth). Scholars say Egypt, or at least Alexandria, was supposed to be a Greek concept and territory. It should not matter when the Romans conquered Greece, their territory should have automatically become Rome.

The Romans should have never had to bow to this woman at all if Egypt/Alexandria belonged to the Greeks. Also, why didn't the Romans fight with the Greek against the Persians? By 405 B.C., they all definitely co-existed. It's all quite elementary, the Kingdom of Alexandria in Egypt was completed at least 2,100 years before there was a Greece, a Carthage, or a Rome as Professor Mer-enjiuti declared and the Persian Empire was long defeated.

It is logical to conclude that Greece, Carthage, and Rome were born of the teachings, philosophies, and disciplines of the University of Alexandria, Egypt. Nevertheless, this hesitation of Rome and the length of the uninterrupted bloodline of the Ptolemy's (I-XII) as well as the seven queens named Cleopatra in a time when Egypt was at peace with everyone is an indirect proof to the words of Mer-enjiuti about the age and the position the Kingdom of Alexandria actually held as the capital and ultimate learning center of the Mediterranean World. The Romans were apprehensive because of this legacy of longevity and honor, the kingdom's imposing skyline, magnificent man-made double harbor and bay and the way it lit up at night.

The Kingdom of Alexandria itself was a wonder of the world not just its Lighthouse. The Romans quivered at the thought of taking over Alexandria in 149 B.C. because they were still students and subordinates to the kingdom. So, they hid their true agenda and put their tails between their legs deciding to go north first, take over Greece and present-day France, then later brought their list of demands to a Queen Pharaoh instead of a King Pharaoh. This implies the Romans had malice… the cowards.

*Africa: It's True Role in the Ancient World*

## The Roman Hesitation

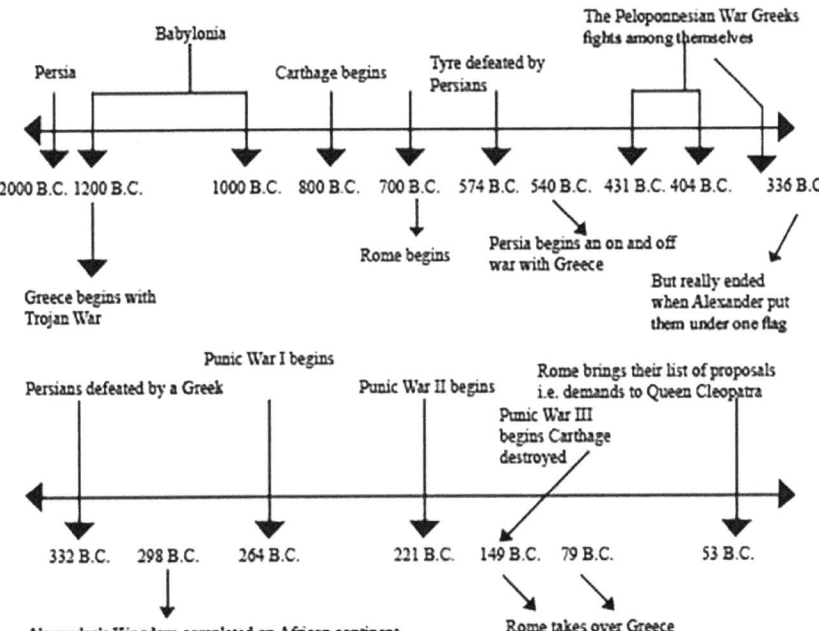

Again, why did the Romans hesitate in 149 B.C. to march in and takeover the Kingdom of Alexandria. They were already on the African continent. They had the supplies and the manpower to do it and they still elected to go back north, across the Mediterranean Sea, wait some 70 years to take over Greece (if they didn't already in 149 B.C. as some scholars say). And then another 25 years during which they took over Gaul, present day France, to return south back across the Mediterranean Sea where they already were in 149 B.C. just to give this list of proposals to a woman that they eventually did not like. The Romans bowed to this woman for 12 years before going to war with her for 7.

I think they could have avoided her 76 years before she was ever born. So there must have been more to the Kingdom of Alexandria than the European is willing to tell. I wonder why they are so secretive when it comes to Egypt. Hmm, I wonder.

According to the European, by 405 B.C., the Egyptians, the Persians, the Greeks, the Romans and the Carthaginians all coexisted. Save perhaps the Greeks, there is no record of the eastern side of the Mediterranean Sea interacting with the western side even though they all had sea worthy ships. This is preposterous.

# SECTION 12

# The Arab Invasion

In 630 A.D., the Arabs noticed that the Romans (Byzantines) were losing power. **So, in 641 A.D.,** they helped the Africans push the Romans out of Africa. Notwithstanding the losses the Kingdom of Alexandria had sustained during the yearlong battle within its borders, the Arabs found that they had captured a kingdom with 4,000 palaces, 4,000 baths and 400 lecture halls. The Arabs, out of fear, then took the place of the Romans and made slaves of the Africans for about 100 years.

Meanwhile, the Arabs became what they called full Muslims and eventually institutionalized slavery. Together the Africans, now converts, and Arabs pushed the Romans deep into Northern Europe. Note the Arab did not become a full Muslim until they entered Egypt and finished the Koran. In the meantime, the Arabs knowledge increased exponentially in the areas of science, mathematics, astronomy, astrology, masonry, philosophy, medicine, music, logic, metaphysics, engineering, ethics, political science, sociology, teaching and literature while they were in Egypt during the early years of their occupation. They learned these subjects from the burned up remains of the Library of Alexandria, which had been rotting like an open infected wound for over 225 years.

Before this time period, the Arabs were a little more than goat and sheepherders. They resurrected the old classics from the Great Library to bolster their virgin empire. If any African scholar could translate these remaining manuscripts into Arabic that African would receive their weight in gold for every translated manuscript. Unfortunately, the Arabs did not have the same interest in preserving the African culture or architecture. They also burned down and dismantled buildings in Alexandria to build their own kingdoms and left the rest to rot and erode. The Arabs are also guilty of stripping the white limestone from the pyramids at Giza to build their palaces and mosques in those kingdoms.

Following this academic advancement of the Arabs, the Great Library was completely burned to the ground after the Koran was completed on African soil in the year 671 A.D. despite the protest of the Arab scholars. The Arab rulers declared that if the information in the Library of Alexandria was not in the Koran then it was false but if it was in the Koran then it was superfluous, the Great Library of Alexandria was completely destroyed. Notice, it took two separate burning attempts from two different groups of people from two different time periods to completely destroy the Library of Alexandria. This is a testament to its overwhelming size and girth. It is also a testament to the generous nature of the African who designed and built the University of Alexandria and then consolidated the African manuscripts to help those who were less fortunate than himself for free.

Meanwhile, on the eastern side of this new Islamic Empire, the famous House of Wisdom was established in Baghdad in the year 830 A.D. where many of these manuscripts from the Library of Alexandria were translated. Over 3,800 manuscripts were estimated to be translated here by the Arabs. This established the foundation for Islamic scholastics. The House of Wisdom had a library, dormitories, science laboratories, engineering laboratories, hospitals and observatories around it making it a university of its own right. Essentially, it was a model of the former university, enduring for over 400 years.

The Kingdom of Baghdad boasted 500,000 citizens, many of whom were scholars, enjoying hot and cold running water, heating and air conditioning, showers and flushing toilets, fountains and hanging gardens while they studied and discovered the concepts of what is known today as Algebra. Unfortunately, for the extreme eastern part of the Islamic Empire, the Mongols, led by Genghis' grandson, Huelegu Khan, conquered all of Iran, including Baghdad during the expansion of their empire in the year 1258 A.D. The Tigris and Euphrates rivers reportedly ran red with the blood of thousands of scholars and many engineering marvels were dismantled. Then those same "red" rivers ran black with the ink of thousands of books. The House of Wisdom was destroyed and it's like was never established in Baghdad again. In spite of this its influence endured in the western part of their empire.

A little earlier, in 711 A.D., the Arabs and Africans, now Muslims, invaded Spain together and in 750 A.D. established the kingdom/ University of Granada, which endured as a learning center for 742 years. This Islamic military force was saturated with 80% Africans; the other 20% was a mixture of Arabs and the Jewish set known as the Sephardim. In 1050 A.D., these Muslims established another kingdom in Spain called Salamanca, complete with a university that thrived for 500 years under the co-production of Africans and Arabs. This university became a center of learning with a library that held 700,000 books, the root of which were translated into Arabic and transported from the Great Library of Alexandria. Granada along with the University of Timbuktu in West Africa, which received its written word from the same source and the same army, was solely run by Africans for the same 700-year period. Plus, these three institutions, for about 230 years, were the only learning centers on the earth after the collapse of the extreme east side of their empire in 1258 A.D.

These three learning centers were known for their benevolent governments, their great respect for learning, their libraries, their hot and cold running water, heating and air conditioning, showers, flushing toilets, water fountains, hanging gardens and their trade routes. Timbuktu in Mali was also known for its gold mines. These three Islamic universities marked the Africans third Golden Age since the end of the Ice Age. The first was the 30 Dynasties lasting 2,889 years; the second was the Alexandrian Period lasting more than 3,111 years before Christ and 415 years after his murder and the third and shortest was the Kingdom of Granada together with the universities of Salamanca and Timbuktu lasted for about 780 years. Around the 12th century, the universities of Timbuktu and Salamanca had an attendance of 25,000 and 40,000 students respectively for centuries, in cities that had populations of 100,000 people. Africa's third Golden Age was responsible for bringing the European out of his darkness and into his middle ages and his renaissance period.

The Western European went to school at the Universities of Granada, Salamanca and Timbuktu for 350 years from 1100 A.D. to 1450 A.D. trading and studying with people of color for the second time. Also, not only did the European learn the game of chess here, this is where they learned the art of masonry again and together with the people of color were allowed to roam free along the countryside to build all the castles, temples, and cathedrals in Europe. Scholars say the Knights Templar financed this new construction in stone.

The African professors at these universities taught geography from globes, the European said, and even after teaching the Europeans in Spain for 700 years, the Spanish still believed the world was flat. (You will discover in your research that a good portion of the 14 Black Freemasons in America during the Revolutionary War came from Europe. The others were already in America).

In 1360 A.D., the European made the first gun; an idea he copied from the Islamic hand cannon, and 80 years later began making his West African hosts into slaves in the year 1442 A.D. The second round of slavery, by the hands of the Europeans, was sanctioned by the Roman Catholic Pope himself who sent the Good Ship Jesus, the Grace of God and the Holy Mary owned by the Jewish people known as the Sephardim to collect the Africans, 800 at a time in each ship. The Arabs institutionalized slavery and the Europeans industrialized it for another 423 years. During this second round of European slavery against his host, 150,000,000 Africans died on the way over to the Americas. Africans did not just fall at the feet of the European invaders, no; they fought fiercely, bravely, and continuously.

Armed resistance sprung up all over West Africa. The Zulu Wars lasted from the 1650's A.D. to 1906 A.D. and in Ghana, the Ashanti Wars lasted from 1710 A.D. to the last battle fought in 1900 A.D. This means that the Africans were being kidnapped in large numbers for 200 years before the Africans unified and fought against the European lusts for human souls. The European is truly the father of the lie. By 1884 A.D. there was no question as to who ruled Africa; it was a question of what region.

Still later that century, to rid the European peninsula of the intelligent dark people, the Roman Catholic Pope sanctioned the Spanish Inquisition in the year 1478 A.D. which lasted for 350 years. During this time period, the Europeans tortured and burned 100,000 women, tortured and burned 35,000 men and displaced 250,000 Muslims from the peninsula of Europe in an attempt to keep Europe ignorant, white and Roman Catholic. By 1492 A.D., the Europeans engineered the downfall of the last stronghold of the Moorish Empire known as the Kingdom of Granada. In the court yard of this kingdom the European burned over 700,000 books from the Islamic Empire in Spain claiming that since these books are written in Arabic they are all Korans and therefore evil and must be destroyed. This is the second massive book burning campaign by the European since the last one in Egypt 1,077 years earlier. Unfortunately, it was not the last.

These displaced Muslims settled on the coast of North Africa, which was still a part of their empire at the time. Upset by being kicked out of Spain, i.e. Europe, the Arabs and Africans began building ships to terrorize the European trade routes in the Mediterranean Sea. These Muslims pirated so much treasure that some of the European Christians and Jews converted to Islam just to get their hands on some of the loot. The North African coast, now the Barbary Coast had boundaries that stretched from Egypt in the east to the Atlantic Ocean in the west. It was named after the Berber which is a term describing the Moors who are again, black people. It was also short for barbarian. That's how ruthless the displaced Muslims became; the true barbarian called the Muslims from that part of the world barbarous.

The Europeans feared the coast of North Africa for more than 300 years from 1490 A.D. to 1830 A.D. The Muslims soon discovered that kidnapping the European sailors and merchants for ransom was more lucrative than just killing them. Not much later, these Muslim pirates began making the European into slaves. They terrorized and kidnapped European men, women and children as far north as the British Isles. It has been estimated that during this 300-year period over 1,000,000 Europeans were made into slaves, forced to build for the Muslims the largest palace in the Northern Hemisphere. This palace is somewhere in Northeastern Morocco.

In the 1800's, the newly formed America and the European powers, France, Spain and England stopped fighting among themselves long enough to ban together and stop the pirating by colonizing the Barbary Coast. In 1805 A.D., the U.S. Marines fought at Tripoli in North Africa to gain control of their interest in the trade routes. They wore leather around their necks to prevent decapitation from the Arabian Sabers hence the name "Leather Necks." The Tripoli battle was so important, so inspiring that it made it into the Marine Corporations fight song. "From the Halls of Montezuma (in Mexico) to the shores of Tripoli (**in North Africa**)." When the European made his way into North Africa to liberate his captured enslaved citizens, the European female was reluctant to return to Europe with him. She enjoyed her role in the harem and was treated like a goddess. She knew that upon her return to Europe it was back to Victorianism and third-class citizenship. Remember, chivalry comes from the Islamic world, not the European world.

What is most remarkable is that both the Universities of Salamanca and Timbuktu still exist today. The difference is that Salamanca is no longer co-produced by Africans and Arabs, Timbuktu is no longer run strictly by Africans and both are shells of their former selves. One more thing, unlike the Byzantine Empire, the Kingdoms of Granada, Salamanca and Timbuktu had no walls and they all coexisted for at least 430 years. The people of the Kingdoms of Granada, Salamanca and Timbuktu offered their knowledge freely and with open arms while the Europeans hid their stolen information for 1,100 years behind walls.

Note that the Eastern Europeans (Byzantines) are the only group of people who had the knowledge of the Egyptians. The Western Europeans did not, but the people of Timbuktu, Granada and Salamanca actually had the Egyptian. Meanwhile, Western Europe collapsed into darkness whereas Timbuktu, Granada and Salamanca enjoyed the same standard of living the Byzantines did. So, who really needs whom here?

In 1884 A.D. the European finally had control of Africa and divided it up among European territories. It took the European 1,918 years to acquire the continent of Africa for himself. It was 1,918 years from the time of Queen Cleopatra's forced suicide to the 1884 A.D. carving of the richest continent of the world. I have come to three distinct conclusions about the African, other than the fact that the African is the founder of civilization and all religious systems. First; the African is benevolent and generous in nature, second; the African does not build a civilization without a university at its center, and third; the African has been a slave for over 1,000 years.

## The Islamic Empire

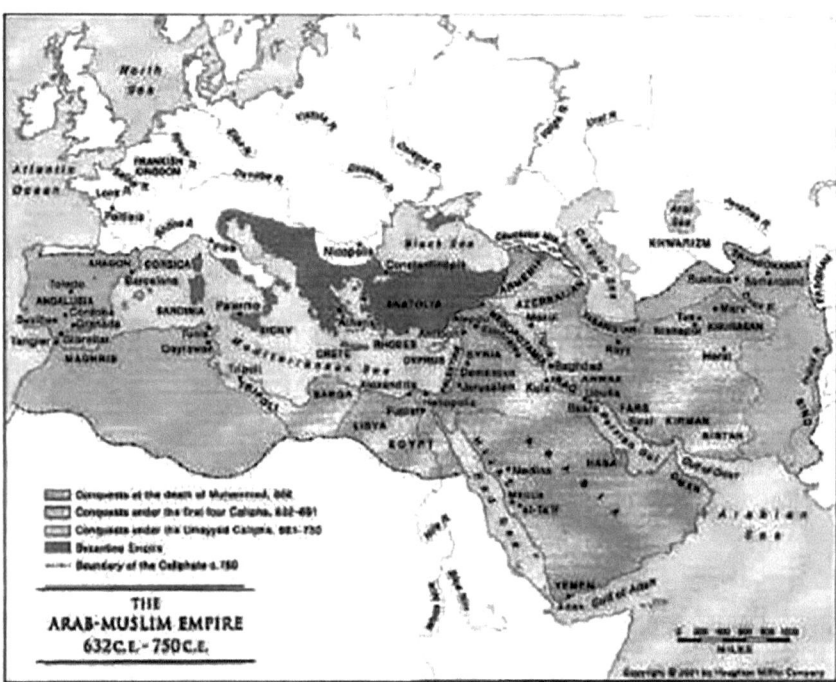

This is the extent of the Islamic Empire. Note that their ranks in their army were saturated with African converts as they swept across North Africa into Spain. 100 years later, the House of Wisdom was established in Baghdad.

# SECTION 13

# European Saviors: Granada, Salamanca, Timbuktu and the Rosetta Stone.

# The Significance of the Zodiac

People say that the European's Renaissance Period has its roots in literature, architecture, sculpture and painting. However, there is another form of Renaissance that occurred in this time period from 1453 A.D. to 1749 A.D. that scholars don't like to discuss outside of their inner circles. The schools of France, Italy and England became universities when the teachers finished their studies in Timbuktu, Granada and Salamanca and became philosophers. The teachers began to think critically about their condition, their roots and why they became philosophers in the first place.

These new renaissance philosophers knew about the Christians, the Byzantines, the Muslims, the Romans, the Greeks and the so-called Greek contribution to western civilization. Then these new philosophers began to look at the contributions of the Greek philosophers themselves after the Byzantine Empire collapsed, making the bulk of their manuscripts available to Western Europe. As to be expected, one of these new renaissance philosophers counted the contribution of each Greek philosopher to honor those philosophers for bringing the renaissance philosophers into the light of self-comprehension while at the same time denying the master teachers at the universities of Granada, Salamanca and Timbuktu ever taught them.

These renaissance philosophers found out that there was only ten Great Greek Philosophers with 2,000 manuscripts accredited to them. That means on average each Greek philosopher wrote 200 manuscripts and some are accredited with writing 400 manuscripts. These 2,000 manuscripts run the gamut of all the-ology's, all the engineering sciences, all the mathematics, all the chemistry, all the medical fields and everything the renaissance philosophers Nostradamus, Newton, Leibniz, Copernicus, and Galileo, just to name a few, are accredited for discovering. It was at this point the Europeans realized that Pythagoras, Socrates, Plato, Aristotle, Hippocrates, and Euclid were only six of the Great Greek philosophers; this means that they had to write a huge portion of the sample space of 2,000 manuscripts.

Moreover, the Europeans realized after trying to write their own manuscripts that it took years to write down just a theorem on a blank sheet of paper from scratch. The Europeans knew that these manuscripts that the Greeks supposedly wrote were not romance novels, short stories, folklore, poetry, musicals, operas, scripts, essays or fiction. These manuscripts were of mathematics and science and therefore could not have been written by the Greeks at all. Again, the Europeans discovered that it is a mathematical impossibility for these ten Great Greek Philosophers to write these 2,000 manuscripts given their short life spans. This is because the European, during his renaissance period, understood the true nature of academics. He discovered that time is required to master any subject, especially mathematics and science.

This is why academic subjects are called disciplines because discipline is required to master them. So, they had no choice but to look elsewhere. Like the detectives we know they can be, they had to be objective about the situation and the undeniable evidence against the Greeks as the bringers of knowledge. They had to swallow their pride and use deductive and inductive reasoning before they remembered that the Library of Alexandria was in Africa. It is at this point the European stopped in his tracks and dropped to his knees in horror and screamed, "God, no! Those niggers are our masters!" (It should be noted that all of the renaissance philosophers studied alchemy or alkemy. Alkemy comes from the word al-kemi, which means "the way of Kemet or Egypt". Egypt is a word from the Greek that describes the land of the valley the Africans called Kemet. So, these scholars knew where the knowledge originated. And they covered this secret with the code word "alchemy". Throughout history, alchemy, has been known as a pseudo-science of turning base metals into gold. Now, through this code word, we know that these philosophers claimed the works and academic accomplishments of the Africans as their own).

The evidence the European discovered about Africa implies too many things about the African, things that do not make the European look good at all so they dismissed this conjecture for as long as they could. This 200-year-old legend finally spread throughout Europe and the evidence, in the Africans favor of being the professors and master teachers of the Greeks and the Romans, as well as the creators of western civilization, could no longer be ignored and a philosopher decided to swallow his pride and find out the truth for himself. He had to wait until the French revolution made it possible for that to happen for him. Soon after, he targeted the Roman Catholic Church and its inquisitions against enlightenment. The church was all but destroyed by this man's invasion.

Then in 1798 A.D., Napoleon Bonaparte was finally able to take 165 philosophers and 50 artisans from Europe back to Africa, specifically the Nile Valley. They went there to find out the truth about themselves, the African and the positions they held with respect to one another in the past. I wonder how many of them were a part of the Masonic Order or even idiot savants for that matter? Nevertheless, these 215 passengers left their pride and superiority complexes on the ships as Napoleon commanded them to. He wanted them to open their minds to the truth about Africa and its mystery systems so they could add whatever breakthrough knowledge they discovered to their present understanding and possibly improve their own conditions.

The goal of this Napoleon group of philosophers and artisans, known as "The Fathers of Egyptology", was to find a way to read the gibberish written on the walls everywhere in Africa. By accident, this group of Egyptologists found a stone tablet in the Nile Delta, 25 miles east of Alexandria in an ancient city named Rosetta. The stone tablet was later named the Rosetta Stone. The Rosetta Stone was engraved with three languages written on it. One language, which was at the top, was Medu-Netcher, the African gibberish, the other in the middle, Demotic, was a cursive form of the Medu-Netcher and the bottom was Greek. The three languages were written in the same text. This text was a story about Ptolemy V. Note that if Alexander the Great conquered Egypt and made it a Greek territory then why is the Greek language at the bottom of the Rosetta Stone? Again, it is because Egypt was liberated and made sovereign again by Alexander the Great and his Greek people were nothing but students of Egypt, bringing nothing of significance to the equation of knowledge.

Furthermore, the Rosetta Stone was written during the reign of Ptolemy V. This means that after five generations of Ptolemaic rule, the dominant language was still the Egyptians. I wonder how long a generation is especially when there are supposed to be only 290 years between Ptolemy I and Queen Cleopatra VII, last Egyptian Pharaoh, daughter of Ptolemy XII.

With espionage, the French, the Spanish and the English fought each other to get a copy of this stone. The reason being is that the Europeans did not want Napoleon to upset the balance of power with some new scientific breakthrough that could be used as a weapon to take over the world. From 1812 A.D. to 1821 A.D., the European powers hunted Napoleon down and killed him for exposing the greatness that is black to the world. Back in 1800 A.D., all three countries finally had a copy of the stone. Now, the race was on to see which country could decipher it first. 21 years later, a Frenchman named Jean Francois Champollion deciphered the stone and the English held him in the highest regards, honoring him with several doctoral degrees then later sent him up the Nile in style.

The French could not send the Frenchman up the Nile because the French were bankrupt. They spent all their money building palaces, canals and with Ben Franklin to help the Americans in their Revolutionary War against France's rivals, the English. This Frenchman was allowed to decipher the Africans language to his heart's content. 62 years later, more than the average life span of a European at that time, America did not just turn on an experimental electric light on a table and then celebrate with champagne. No! They turned on a square mile of New York City's downtown Manhattan Island with electricity in 1883 A.D. at night so there would be no doubts and President Chester A. Author was there to pull the switch. It is the only thing he is famous for.

The 19$^{th}$ century is the Europeans scientific breakthrough century in which he made leaps and bounds in the areas of mathematics, science and technology. The European has made you think this is a coincidence, that the deciphering of the Egyptian language was just academic research and curiosity and had no effect on the exponential growth in his knowledge base; assuming that you know anything about the Rosetta Stone and its history to begin with. What do you think?

I say the Europeans turned on the first hydroelectric plant in America 1,917 years after the one in Africa, which powered the Lighthouse of Alexandria and the kingdom, was turned off by Queen Cleopatra. Careers were dedicated to making this particular Egyptian mystery system, among others, a reality for the European today. So, even if you could reject the contributions the Rosetta Stone has with respect to electricity and the explosion of knowledge in other applied math and sciences to produce this modern world we live in today, Thomas Edison still could not have accomplished the feat of electricity without the help of an African named Lewis Latimer who made electricity's use practical.

Despite what we have been told for centuries, it has been documented today that the Egyptians never had slaves. So what kind of power source did the Africans have that the Europeans needed slavery to equal, and I use the word equal loosely, that they no longer needed slavery after deciphering and reading the African's language? Meanwhile, back in Egypt, because of exasperation, Napoleon not only blew off the ethnic nose of the Sphinx, he also dismantled a beautiful ceiling relief from the Temple of Dendera to take back to Europe. He had no idea what he had. It turns out that this ceiling relief is the Zodiac Calendar. This calendar is a clock that measures the 24 hours of the day, the day of the 10-day week, the week of the 3-week month, the month of the 12-month year and the 12 signs of the zodiac. This calendar is a perfect clock, even today, that takes into account that the year is precisely 365.2422 days.

What is most exciting is that scientists today have discovered that it takes 26,000 years to complete one zodiac cycle. To be specific the zodiac cycle is known as the Great Year. The Great Year is caused by a slight wobble of the earth's axis caused by the gravitational pull of the sun and moon at the equator. This gravitational pull is also responsible for the equatorial bulge that makes the earth wider at the equator than at the poles. This unequal distribution of mass causes the earth to wobble around its rotational axis like a gyroscope. What this means is the earth's axis makes its own rotation.

This slight wobble takes an estimated 26,000 years to complete one cycle. This wobble is responsible for the Great Year and its apparent movement through the 12 signs of the zodiac. The Great Year should not be confused with the yearly cycle or solar year in which the people of the Nile named the same 12 constellations in the sky to keep track of events that happen on earth within the seasons every year. A good example of which is on the very globe today: the tropic of Cancer and the tropic of Capricorn. The tropics are imaginary lines of latitude that are parallel to the equator and run 23.5 degree north and south of the equator respectively. These two imaginary lines of latitude are the boundaries for the ecliptic, which is another imaginary line that depicts the path of the earth around the sun or the plane in which the path of the sun is located on earth.

This path is represented by the ecliptic line tilted 23.5 degrees with respect to the Equator. Now the sun is at its highest point in the sky on June 21st and is represented on the ecliptics furthest point north. At this time the constellation named Cancer is in the sky thus the name "Tropic of Cancer".

On December 21st the sun is at its lowest point in the sky with respect to the northern hemisphere and is represented on the ecliptics furthest point south, at this time the constellation Capricorn is in the sky thus the name "Tropic of Capricorn". The phrase, "Endless Summer", exists between the tropics.

The 12 signs of the zodiac are the same constellations the Egyptians named that follow and align themselves with the ecliptic. This apparent movement through the Great Year, however, is categorized by the sun rising over the equator on the date of the spring equinox, March 21st, directly underneath a different zodiac sign. A phenomenon that occurs every 2,160 years, 12 times 2,160 is 25,920 or approximately 26,000 years. Each 2,160-year period is called an age or eon.

Pisces is the age we are currently in now, 1 A.D. to 2160 A.D., its symbol is two fish, remember Christianity used to be symbolized by two fish or a fish before the crucifix, this is the reason why. Before this age it was the age of the Ram (Aries) about 2160 B.C. to 1 A.D. It is the real reason why the Jewish people blow the rams horn in their celebrations. The Jews are celebrating their freedom from bondage in Egypt. Before this age was the age of the Bull (Taurus) around 4320 B.C. to 2160 B.C., remember the story, 3,000 Jewish people were killed by Moses for worshipping and dancing around the golden Bull calf after he came down out of the mountains. Moses represents the end of this age and the start of the Rams age. This is why he was so upset with the people. (The story of Moses is a myth, which means it never happened, it was written to give the Jewish people something positive to believe in after they were thrown out of Egypt by the Pharaoh Ahmose I of the 18th Dynasty because they are the Hyksos).

The Hyksos are the people that declared themselves Jews after they left what is now known as the middle-east and settled in present day Poland. They did this to get away from Islam and Christianity during the Islamic invasion around 600 A.D. They did not want to be Christians or Muslims so they took a little of both, put their own twist on the result and called it Judaism as well as calling themselves Jews and the true descendants of Abraham around 800 A.D. Originally, they are from the Caucus Mountains. Note, they called themselves Jews way after Egypt and Jesus. This implies that they wrote all that stuff in the Bible about themselves after the fact.

Again, the Hyksos were invaders who established the 13th Dynasty and remained in the Nile Delta until Ahmose I threw them out. Fortunately, this happens to be the same time that Abraham enters into Egypt, (Genesis 12:10-11). There may be some debate about this but one thing is certain, the pharaoh did <u>give</u> the princess Hagar to Abraham because Genesis 12:20, 13:1 and 16:1 imply it. Any indigenous pharaoh would <u>never</u> give an African daughter to a foreigner because the pathway to the throne was always through the black woman. She was considered a goddess and treated as such. Remember, the Egyptian had both the patriarchal and the matriarchal systems: a system of duality like the yin and yang. Specifically, for Osiris and Isis. The Jews and Romans omitted the matriarchal in favor of the masculine and logic making the female a second-class citizen i.e. (Hagar the handmaid). This is why scholars know the throne of Egypt was ruled by an invader at the time of Abraham and those invaders had to be the Hyksos. This means Abraham, Isaac, Jacob and Joseph came into the Nile Delta at a time when there were no indigenous Africans on the throne. Note, the Arabs trace their lineage back to the union of Abraham and Hagar.

The Jewish scholars know who they are and they know Moses never lived plus there was no slavery in Africa by the hands of the Africans. Indeed, if the European Jew was really a slave in Egypt for 400 years as he declares then he would no longer exist. The

African would have mated him out of existence. They also forgot their supposed 400 years of bondage in Egypt when they arrogantly told Jesus "We are Abraham's descendants, and have never been in bondage to anyone." John (8:1-59). Note that Jesus did not remind them of their bondage in Egypt. It's because it never happened. Or did Jesus forget too? Or is it that he was afraid to remind them? Again, they are the Hyksos who, by all accounts, were actually enslaving the African in the land of Egypt for 265 years. Repayment after the African clothed and fed him. They are the ones that have quietly concluded that Moses never lived and their enslavement in Egypt never happened. This revelation occurred in the 1990's among their secret hierarchy of Rabbi's documented in their own intellectual magazines and newspapers. These Jews were so upset at the African for kicking them out of Egypt that around 550 A.D. they wrote the Ham story in their written laws called "The Babylonian Talmud" which made it into the Bible. Remember the cursed sons of Ham Genesis (9: 20-29). Genesis (10: 6) and the sons of Ham were Kush (Ethiopia), Mizraim (Egypt), Phut (Somalia) and Cannon (present day Israel), cursed black because these were the names of the Blackman's land on the Genesis map of the world after the flood. Moreover, the Babylonia Talmud is much more explicit pertaining to the cursed sons of Ham. It actually says they are cursed black (Chapter 9:25-27). They wrote this story to justify the taking of the land of Cannon about four thousand years earlier according to Mer-enjiuti; Deuteronomy 7 as well as Joshua 10, 11 and 12.

The Jews wrote this and the blacks believed it. This is just one example of mental and spiritual control over the remaining Africans and it endures in the minds of the Africans to this day. The Jews also wrote about themselves to make themselves benevolent or "The Chosen People". Genesis (10: 2) and the sons of Japheth were Gomer, Magog, Madal, Javan, Tubal, Meshech and Tiras all in Eastern Europe if you are lucky enough to see the Genesis map of the world after the flood today.

And one of the sons of Gomer was Ashkenaz, 80% of the Jews consider themselves Ashkenazim and Ashkenaz is the Caucus

Mountains, the other 20% of the Jewish people are the Sephardim. (Again, for more clarity, Genesis (9:25-27) the sons of Ham shell serve the sons of Japheth).

For your edification the Ethiopian Jews do not have the Ham story in their holy scriptures. They took the original text deep into Ethiopia to Axum to prevent it from being destroyed by the Romans in the year 44 A.D. The Romans were on a rampage, attempting to rid the world of the original Christian doctrines along with the original Christians themselves. The book is still safe in Ethiopia today.

It should be noted that the first age was the lion (Leo) about 10800 B.C. to 8650 B.C. The Sphinx is supposed to represent the dawning of this age. This implies that the Sphinx was fashioned before this age in preparation for its arrival. Two hard sciences prove beyond any doubt that the Sphinx is at most 13,000 years old. These two hard sciences are Astronomy and Geology. The New Age Egyptologists say the Sphinx is 19,500 years old. The sciences of Astronomy and Geology say the Sphinx is at most 13,000 years old. In either case these dates are immense compared to the conservative date of 4,500 years old declared by the European for the age of this great statue.

It is interesting that Leo is the first age when clearly the sky clock did not start in that constellation. The earth is at least 4.5 billion years old so there has to be another reason for Leo being the first age. Based on the evidence and the recurring date of 13,000 years ago, I believe that Leo is called the first age because it is the age when the last Crustal Displacement or Polar Shift took place.

The new age we are entering in is the Age of Aquarius, peaking in 2160 A.D. when the sun rises over the equator directly underneath this zodiac sign on March 21$^{st}$ of that year. For your edification, the wobble of the earth is also responsible for the nine North Pole stars as reported by the Egyptians through their paintings and writings. The current pole star is Polaris the next pole star is...

The fundamental reason why we have the knowledge of the zodiac and the nine Polar star system is because of the magnificent Africans who recorded this information with stories in the stars many, many eons ago. The Africans did this for the purpose of survival. Moreover, the Great Year goes through the signs of the zodiac in reverse order from the solar cycle. This phenomenon is known as the precession of the equinoxes; the solar cycle (Capricornus to Sagittarius) takes 365 days. The Great Year (Sagittarius to Capricornus) takes 25,920 years. One more thing, it is the apparent movement of the sun through the course of a year that is responsible for the dates of Christmas and Easter. For Christmas we are really celebrating the birth of the S-U-N and its first step in returning to the northern hemisphere on December 25$^{th}$. Again, on December 21$^{st}$ the sun is at its lowest point in the sky with respect to the northern hemisphere it stays at its lowest point for three days December 22$^{nd}$, 23$^{rd}$ and 24$^{th}$ residing in the vicinity of the Crux constellation, also called the "Southern Cross" only to rise one degree north on December 25$^{th}$. Thus, it is said, "The sun died on the cross, stayed dead for three days only to rise again". You can verify this by following the ecliptic line on the globe.

As for Easter we are actually celebrating its arrival and with it the renewal of life (Spring/Summer). The Europeans/Romans corrupted these sacred events for the purpose of separating the public from nature and thus, each other. He did this for political and social control do to the fact that they were losing control militarily. It should be understood that Easter is never or very rarely on the same date like Christmas is.

We usually celebrate Easter at most 7 days after the first full moon after the spring equinox when the sun has truly passed over the equator and is in the northern hemisphere. The reason Easter is very rarely celebrated on the same day like Christmas is, there are 13 full moons a year not 12; 52 weeks a year divided by 4 weeks per full moon is 13. That is why. We are definitely not celebrating the angel of death passing over the Jewish people's huts in Egypt; this is a part of the same continuing myth. We are also not celebrating the crucifixion, three-day death and rise of Jesus Christ because, if you are counting, there has never been three days between Good Friday (the day of crucifixion) and Easter Sunday (the day of resurrection) you will be surprised at how deep the level of corruption really is.

Many people believe that the world is going to end on December 21st 2012 A.D. (and if the Sumerians are correct about what they call Nibiru, our world will probably change dramatically around that date) but what is known for sure is, this date will usher in the dawning of the Age of Aquarius. This dawning of a new age occurs when the sun rises on a specific day directly between two constellations. Still what is most fascinating is that on December 21st 2012 A.D. the sun, earth and moon will line up with the galactic center of our galaxy the Milky Way. This aligning of the galactic center, the sun, earth and moon happens every 26,000 years or so. Because of the wobble of the earth, the sun, as it appears from the horizon, rises south of the galactic center, then in front of the galactic center, then north of the galactic center. This cycle or oscillation of passing back and forth in front of the galactic center takes 26,000 years. Unfortunately, I am unaware of what happened to the earth the last time this phenomenon occurred, 26,000 years ago.

This knowledge is not new or modern-day knowledge it has been known throughout the ancient world as common knowledge, for without it there is no harvest and no life. This knowledge would imply that the African team that put this clock together would have had to memorize the sky. Like a person today trying to memorize a rap song, it would take at least 16 cycles of the song to remember the words let alone everything else that makes the song unique. That would mean that it took the people of the Nile at least 416,000 years to memorize the cycles of the sky clock, and then put this perfect zodiac clock on a ceiling as a relief in the Temple of Dendera. Imagine the technology the Africans must have had to accomplish this daunting feat.

I cannot stress this enough. The Egyptians had first to be aware that there was a pattern in the sky to pay attention to in the first place. Then, take the time to watch the pattern in the sky slowly tick by. They also had the presence of mind to determine its cause. This is a testament to the ingenuity and longevity of the African. One more thing, if the African spent that much time and put that much devotion in a clock, imagine what kind of homes we lived in, what kind of societies we created, what kind of kingdoms we built in Africa. I would say nothing short of paradise. It should be noted that the European has not left the Nile Valley since his return in 1798 A.D.

The African presents in Spain (and in Europe for that matter) was so influential that the Europeans who studied there, especially the ones from France, Italy and England, founded their own universities. Again, the founders of these universities all studied at the feet of Africans just like the Greeks did in Egypt. The founding dates and names of these countries famous institutions of higher learning include but are not limited to: in 1158 A.D. The University of Bologna, in 1180 A.D. The University of Montpellier, in 1200 A.D. Oxford University, in 1223 A.D. The University of Toulouse, in 1224 A.D. The University of Naples, in 1228 A.D. The University of Padua, in 1245 A.D. The University of Rome and in 1257 A.D. Cambridge University. You may have heard of some of these European universities named here, like Oxford at least. I suggest that you look them up on the internet and marvel at their grandeur while knowing that they would not exist without the teachings, lectures and guidance the founders received from the African for free.

## The Greek Philosophers

The first 5 of the 10 Great Greek Philosophers are:

1. Pythtagoras         560 B.C. to 480 B.C. 80 yrs. old
2. Socrates            470 B.C. to 399 B.C. 71 yrs. old
3. Hippocrates         460 B.C. to 377 B.C. 83 yrs. old
4. Plato               427 B.C. to 347 B.C. 80 yrs. old
5. Aristotle           384 B.C. to 322 B.C. 62 yrs. old

Average age of the first five Great European Philosophers = 75.2 years old

These gentlemen are half of the great Greek philosophers so it can be assumed that they wrote half of the Greek collection of academic writings. That is half of a collection of 2,000 manuscripts. That is 200 manuscripts, on average, for each philosopher. This is impossible considering the fact that during their life times, the Greeks were at war with the Persians, 540 B.C. to 332 B.C. ending with Alexander the Great, and they were at war with themselves, the Peloponnesian war 431 B.C. to 336 B.C. when Alexander put them under one flag. Plus, all the Greek children by age 7 had to study military tactics for at least 10 years to make them fighters because of the decline of the male population due to all the warring. Not to mention that these manuscripts were of mathematics, physics, medicine, engineering, ethics, logic, science, astronomy, music, metaphysics, political science, sociology, teaching and literature. As you can see, the Greeks did not live long enough to learn this material and then write these manuscripts. So, they had to go somewhere else to learn something else.

The only place they could have gone to learn is Egypt. It should be noted that the second 5 of the 10 Great Greek Philosophers all studied in the Kingdom of Alexandria, Egypt.

Napoleon I
Emperor of the French

"Ambition is never content, even on the summit of greatness." *Napoleon Bonaparte*

Napoleon Bonaparte and his fleets

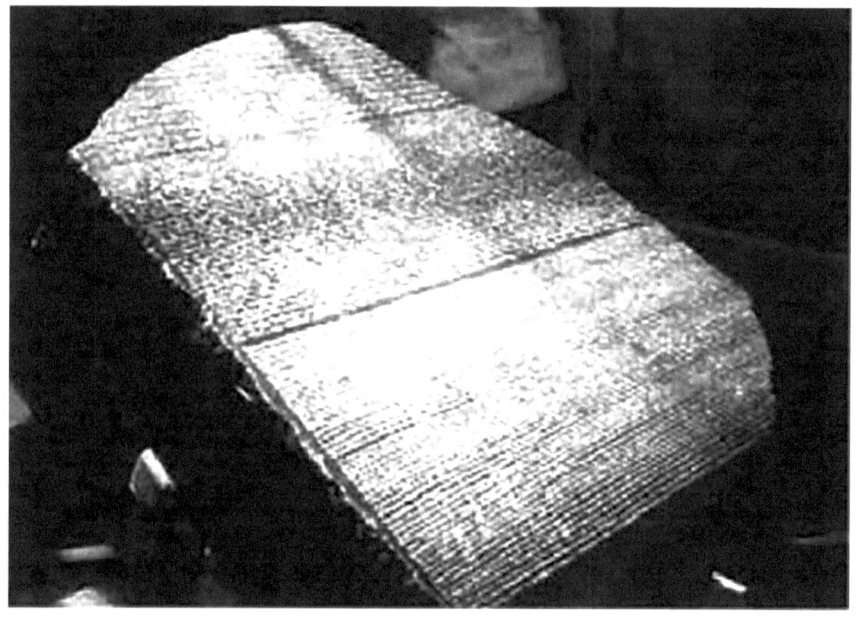

THE MOST IMPORTANT FIND OF ALL TIME

The Yearly Path of the Earth through the 12 Signs of the Zodiac. Notice that the Earth is closer to the Sun in the winter.

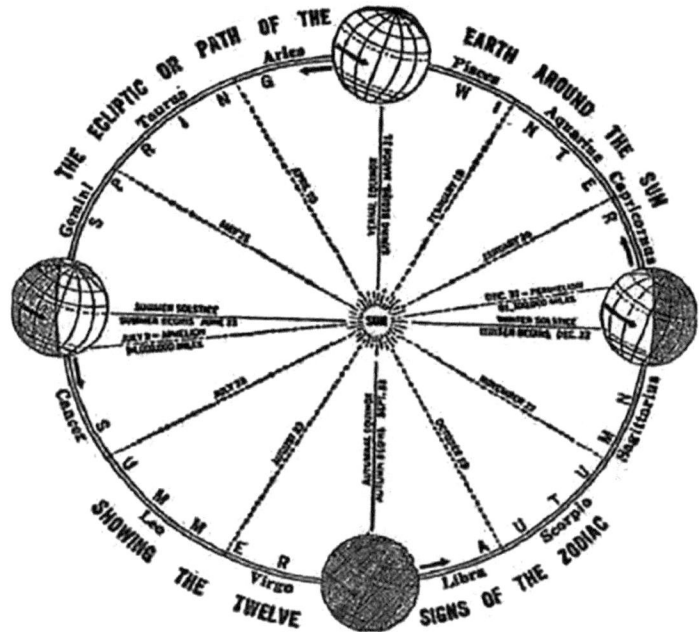

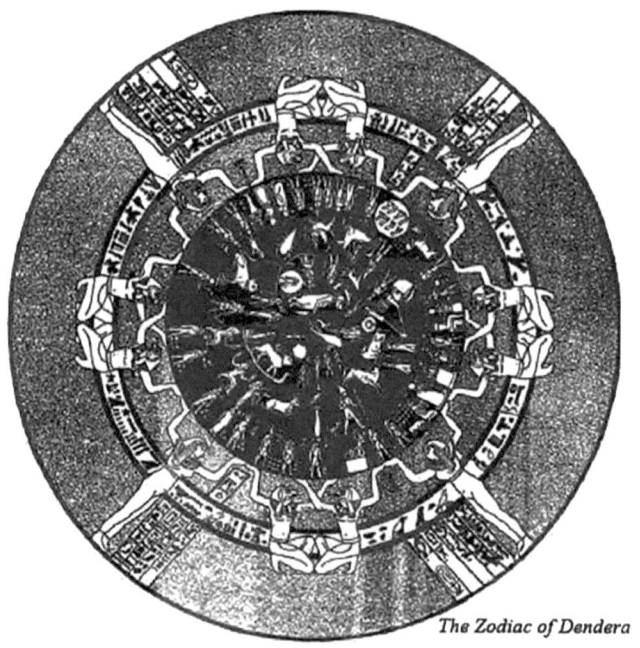

*The Zodiac of Dendera*

The original zodiac was located in the ceiling of an observatory at the Temple of Dendera. It was discovered by Napoleon's troops in 1799 A.D. and dynamited from the ceiling. After a series of owners, it was sold to Louise XVII for 150,000 francs and is now located in the Louvre Museum. The inner circle of figures, which move counter clockwise like the stars, shows the astrological signs of the zodiac circling around the North Pole. The North Pole is symbolized by the jackal. The outer circle of figures represents 36 decans, each one symbolizes the ten-day weeks of the Egyptian year. The 12 figures outside of the circle represent the 12 months of the year and their arms, the 24 hours of the day.

*Africa: It's True Role in the Ancient World*

The Ethiopians of Thebes named the stars of the earth's yearly cycle. Stars of inundation (Aquarius), those stars under which the Nile began to overflow; stars of the ox or bull (Taurus), those under which they began to plow; stars of the lion (Leo), those under which that animal, driven from the desert by thirst, appeared on the banks of the Nile; stars of the sheaf, or of the harvest virgin (Virgo), those of the reaping season; stars of the lamb (Aries), stars of two kids (Gemini), those under which precious life was brought forth. In the same manner he named the stars of the crab, those were the sun, having arrived at the tropics, or highest point in the sky, retreated by a slow retrograde motion back to the southern Hemisphere like a crab (Cancer). He named the stars of the wild goat or (Capricornus), those where the sun, having reached the lowest point in its yearly tract, imitates the goat for it delights to climb back to the summit of the rocks. He named balance (Libra), those where the days and nights are equal, seemed to be in the equilibrium, like that measuring instrument the scale; and the stars of the (Scorpion), those where certain periodic winds bring vapors, burning like the venom of the Scorpion. The stars of the (Pisces), which follow Aquarius during the course of the earth's yearly cycle indicates the fertilization of the land following the inundation. The fish represents fecundating aspects of the Nile River. The stars (Sagittarius) portray a being with two heads, one looking forward and the other looking backward. It is a symbol associated with the completion of a successful harvest season and the anticipation of a productive harvest next season.

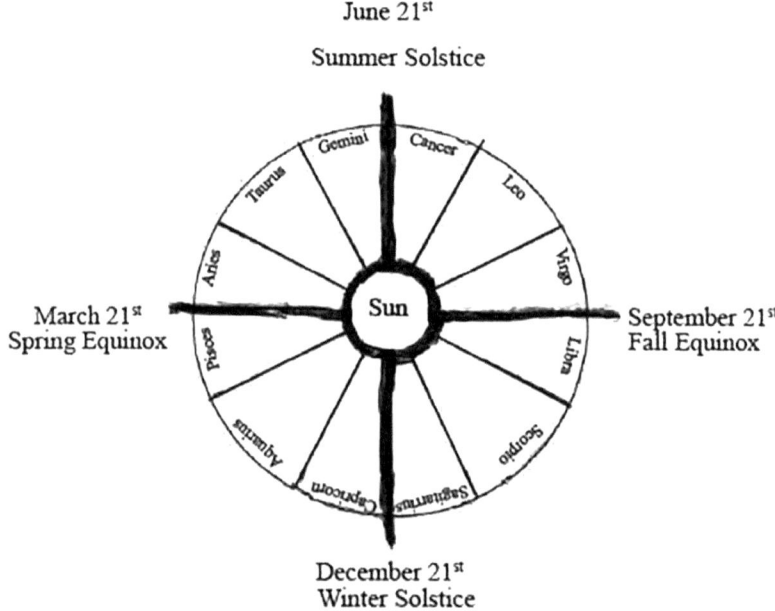

This is the cross of the Zodiac. It is one of the oldest conceptual images in human history. It reflects the sun as it figuratively passes through the 12 major constellations throughout the course of a year.

This is the cross of the Zodiac, adopted and worshipped by the Church. It is considered by the Roman Catholic Church to be pagen and heathen.

The nine polar star system the Africans described is caused by the wobble of the earth's axis. This wobble is also responsible for the Great Year. The earth's wobble takes 26,000 years to complete one cycle.

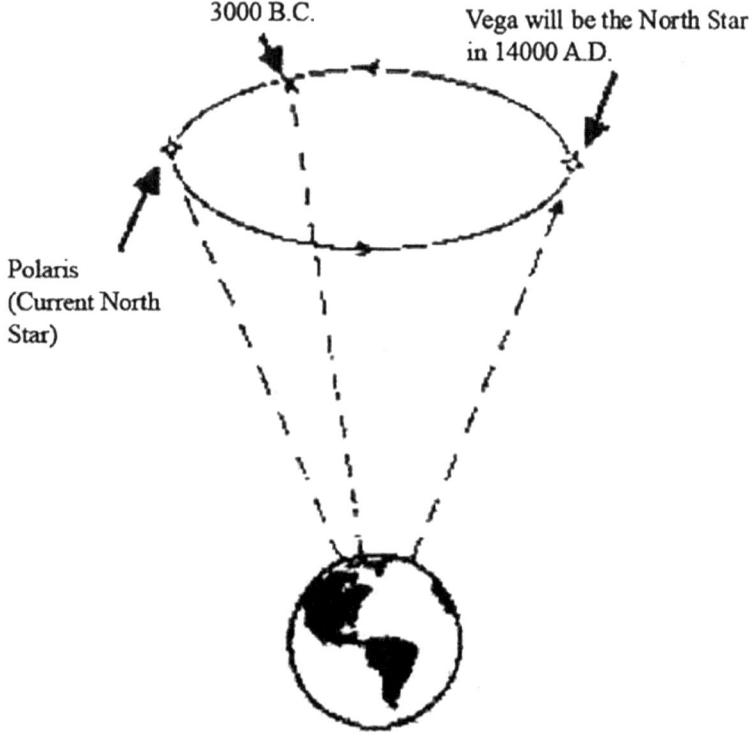

## The Great Year

The earth in its orbit around the sun causes the sun to appear on the celestial sphere and moving over the ecliptic (red line) which is tilted 23.5 degrees from the equator (blue line). The celestial sphere is a projection of the earth's longitude and latitude into space. The celestial sphere is used to map the stars accurately. The wobble of the earth on its axis causes the sun to rise over the equator in a different zodiac constellation every 2,160 years. Notice that the arrow (yellow line) is pointing between Pieces and Aquarius.

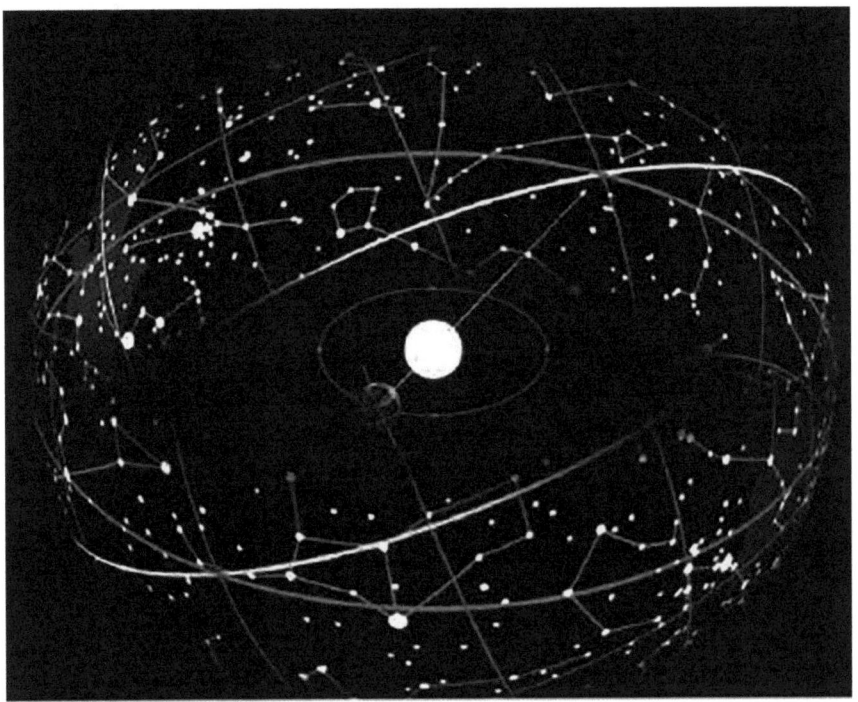

## Our current position in the Great Year

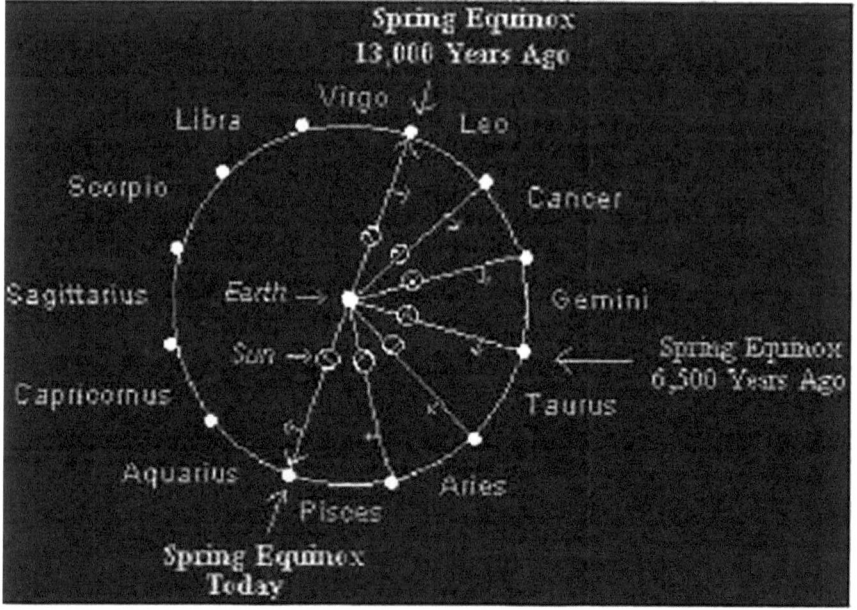

The first age of Leo, dawning on June 21st 10948 B.C. is an example of the sacred knowledge pertaining to the procession of the equinoxes. In the calendar year of the ages of the zodiac, the first Age of Leo dawned on the Summer Solstice. Almost six thousand years later, on

September 21st 4468 B.C., the fourth Age of Taurus dawned on the Autumn Equinox... and so on.

**The Age of Aquarius:
The Water Bearer pouring the Water of Life out of the Urn.**

| | | | |
|---|---|---|---|
| First Age | Age of Leo | dawned in 10948 BCE | Summer Equinox |
| Second Age | Age of Cancer | dawned in 8788 BCE | |
| Third Age | Age of Gemini | dawned in 6628 BCE | |
| Fourth Age | Age of Taurus | dawned in 4468 BCE | Autumn Equinox |
| Fifth Age | Age of Aries | dawned in 2308 BCE | |
| Six Age | Age of Pisces | dawned in 148 BCE | |
| **Seventh Age** | **Age of Aquarius** | **dawns in 2012 AD** | **Winter Equinox** |
| Eighth Age | Age of Capricorn | dawns in 4172 AD | |
| Ninth Age | Age of Sagittarius | dawns in 6332 AD | |
| Tenth Age | Age of Scorpio | dawns in 8492 AD | Spring Equinox |
| Eleventh Age | Age of Libra | dawns in 10652 AD | |
| Twelfth Age | Age of Virgo | dawns in 12812 AD | |

Looking at the precessional cycle of the equinoxes, the "three in one" concept becomes obvious. Within each "Season", there are three ages. Within each "Season" there is a "Trinity" or "Triad of

Ages". Clearly, the primary concern of the people of the Nile was the precession of the equinoxes, and with meticulous care, they encoded the information in the form of paintings, engravings, reliefs and in sculptures. All of the evidence points to the ancient people of the Nile being the progenitors of civilization. They discovered the great secret of procession and its associated geometry. They determined 360 degrees in a circle and created 12 signs of the zodiac, each of 30 degrees. These people also created the constellations of our night sky as their legacy of longevity.

*Africa: It's True Role in the Ancient World* •

The Galactic Alignment
This photo was taken in southern France on July 28, 2008

Note the sun is south of the Milky Way Galaxy in this picture.

This event will occur on December 21, 2012

On the morning of December 21, 2012 A.D., the sun, earth and moon will line up with the galactic center of the Milky Way. Note the 120 degree tilt our horizon has with the Milky Way galaxy (illustrated in the previous picture). It turns out that scientists today, while searching for sources of "dark matter", have discovered that our solar system belongs to another galaxy. This huge sister galaxy circling the Milky Way is called Sagittarius Dwarf Galaxy or SGR for short (red circling line). It is much smaller than the Milky Way, about 10,000 times less massive, and is being consumed by the Milky Way (blue circling line). A new infrared digital survey of the entire sky was made in 2003 A.D. Teams of scientists from the universities of Virginia and Massachusetts used a supercomputer to sort through half a billion stars to create a "New Star Map" showing our solar system (yellow) to be at the exact nexus crossroads where two galaxies are actually joining. The reason for the 120 degree tilt of the Milky Way from the horizon is because our solar system, revolving around the sun, is also revolving in the same plane as the SGR Galaxy and not the Milky Way. Thus, the 120 degree tilt of the Milky Way in our sky. I am sure the ancient civilizations knew this also. If our solar system was a part of the Milky Way Galaxy, then the Milky Way would be perpendicular to the horizon.

# SECTION 14

# 165 Philosophers and 50 Artisans

I have learned that during the lifetimes of those 165 philosophers and 50 artisans that went to Egypt with Napoleon, a 30-volume encyclopedia set, a masterpiece entitled "Description de L'Egypte" was published. This 30-volume encyclopedia set was a scientific and artistic rendition of the sites, buildings, inscriptions, life, language and manners of ancient and modern Egypt. This 30-volume encyclopedia set shattered the myths of the cultural and academic supremacy of the Greeks and established Egypt as the forerunner of all ancient civilizations.

This 30-volume encyclopedia set, where each volume is the size of at least one standard brief case, was started and completed after the rape, burning and pillaging of Alexandria by the hands of the Romans, the rape, burning and dismantling of the remains of Alexandria by the hands of the Arabs. The series of earthquakes from 365 A.D. to 1480 A.D. that toppled the Lighthouse of Alexandria and other tall structures into the Mediterranean Sea plus the 318 more years of rotting, weathering and erosion by the desert sands. In total, the encyclopedia set was written a full 1,400 years after the Romans first burned the Great Library down in 415 A.D. and began their rape of Alexander's Kingdom.

Now, if the Europeans could create a 30-volume encyclopedia set, a masterpiece, after all that destruction, imagine what was there when

Jesus walked the earth one foot in front on the other, when Cleopatra was forced to commit suicide, when the Ptolemaic bloodline was only 1,500 years old. Can you imagine what was there when the Egyptians finished the construction of Alexander's Kingdom; the last stone block was in place and the Ptolemaic family moved in? Can you imagine? I can.

Description de L'Egypt
This illustration is from the Frontispiece

• *Matthew Theodore Momon*

What Napoleon found as he entered Egypt With his 215 scholars

# SECTION 15

# The Black and White I.Q.

With the discovery and deciphering of the Rosetta Stone, it is possible for one to pin point with precision when the Europeans learning curve became a flat line and when it exploded exponentially. The Europeans learning curve descended into hell on average between 415 A.D. to 530 A.D. with the burning of the University of Alexandria and then the fall of Rome, all the way to 1798 A.D. when their knowledge began to increase heavily with the discovery of the Rosetta Stone. In 1822 A.D., after the Rosetta Stone was deciphered, the Europeans gained the modern world, period. Fortunately, this implies that the African continent had the modern world in use before Jesus was murdered and up until the burning of the University of Alexandria 415 years later. Or, at least up until queen Cleopatra's death.

This would imply that the real reason Jesus showed up was on the Africans behalf and not to save us from our sins as we have been told. It is the Romans who had committed the unthinkable, the unnatural not the Africans. Based on the scientific evidence the Africans lived in peace and harmony with each other and the environment. It has been written, like all other profits, Jesus also went to Africa to learn. This implies that the African did not need saving from any sin rather, he needed to be delivered from the Roman.

The Romans betrayed the trust of the African and then seized the modern world from the African after at least 3,111 years of African hospitality and African education. You have to understand that all the sins you know are written on the walls of the Pyramids and Temples of Egypt, all 147 of them, called the Laws of Maat, which were reduced to the 42 Admonishes, then corrupted into the Ten Commandments that you know so well. This implies that the source of those ten sins have less than a 7% representation; in school a score of 7% is a low F.

The original Laws of Maat all started with "I have not". The corrupted Commandments all start with "Thou shalt not". Somehow, we went from a confirmation of self-correctness to a chastising from someone else, and that someone else is not God because God resides within you hence the word "I". The laws of Maat were so well respected and well received by the African that there was no need for a police force. The African had no word for jail because no one had ever gone to one. Additionally, there was no old-folks-home in Africa because no one had ever thrown Grandma and Grandpa away. All this implies that whatever the African was doing before the birth of Christ was alright with God.

Before the European met the African, he was an ignorant Barbarian living in caves. The African later transformed them into thinking men. The European could not see the world through the Africans eyes, he could not see past his five senses to the ultimate true purpose of man, which is to become a god and reach for the infinite potential of the universe. So, he decided to become a beast and betray his master then settle for the earth.

I came into contact with the knowledge that white skin is a trait of the recessive gene, as described by the Punnett square in Biology. The recessive exists in all species. Species that include, but are not limited to, the horse, rhino, buffalo, elephant, lion, tiger, frog, alligator, crocodile, tortoise, and even the plants and insects. White is surprisingly not prevalent in these other species. In fact, white is so infrequent in these species that the Native Americans, Africans and Australians have rituals to celebrate the occasion. So, why is white skin so prevalent in the human species?

It is because it is by design. This is the root of the conspiracy. The Europeans have thought of ways to make this so. The other species cannot think, that is why the white or recessive gets swallowed back up by the black or dominant gene. This is the reason why school is so important. It is also the reason why African Americans receive a substandard education while at the same time being distracted from said education from all sides during the formative years, to keep these facts away from you before you become interested, united and do something about it. The question is what did the Europeans do to make themselves so prevalent in our species? When did they do it? Or did I answer these questions already?

- *Matthew Theodore Momon*

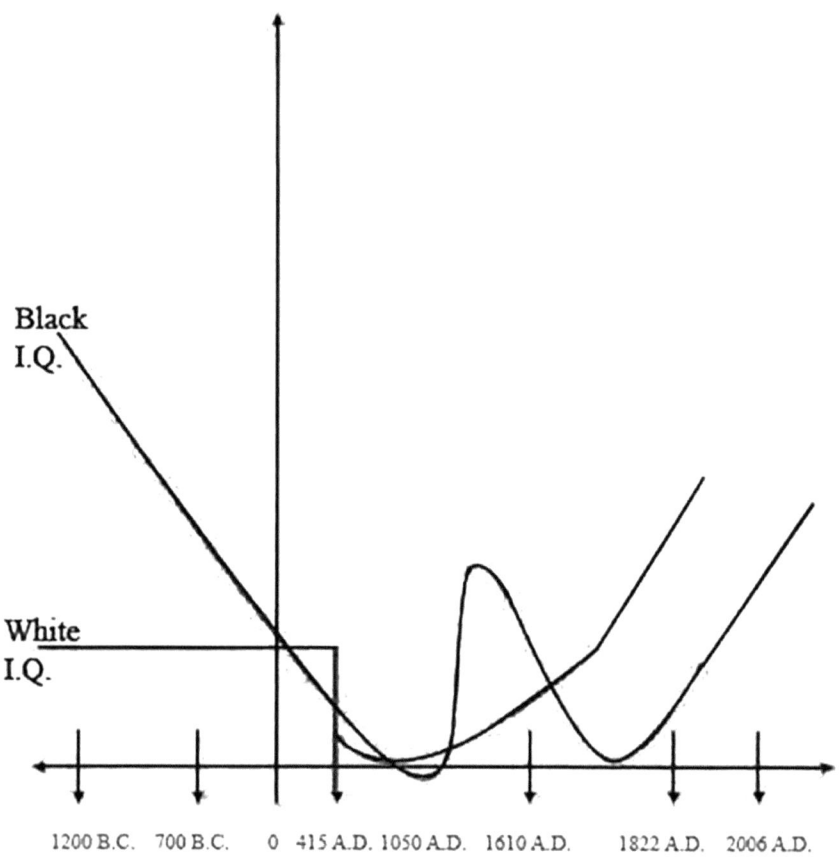

# SECTION 16

# The Nemi Ships

Before the 20th century's WWII, the region of the world where Rome took its last stand in 530 A.D. is literally Germany and Italy today. These modern-day Caesars, Hitler and Mussolini became aware of the fact that Africans had ships powered by wind and steam. The average size ships of 250 feet in length with a 60-foot girth and a 40-foot height could only make port in the Alexandrian Harbor, a harbor that was specially designed for these ships. These ships were large enough that an arena football game could be played on their decks. These ships were too big to make port anywhere else in the Mediterranean World. Today, they are called "The Nemi Ships".

Based on the fact that the Europeans say, the 120-foot long, 19-foot wide and 15-foot high Carthaginian ships weighed 100 tons fully manned and fully loaded. I have calculated that the Nemi Ships had to weigh at least 1,000 tons. Scholars say that many of these super ships were 400 feet long and some were 400-foot long catamarans weighing 4,000 tons, 6,000 tons fully manned and fully loaded. How do you row a 6,000-ton ship?

Back in the 20th century, Mussolini, Dictator of Italy, heard about the 1,500-year-old rumor, a rumor about these kinds of ships that had been built and designed for the Kingdom of Alexandria. They were in use for at least 3,100 years before the Romans decommissioned the ships after joy riding around in them for 500 years like they were theirs. The Romans burned most of the ships of Alexandria and kept two of these average sized ships when they began raping the kingdom. They took the remaining two ships to Italy dismantled them, transported them through Italy, reassembled them, personalized them and then buried then in Lake Nemi near the City of Rome in hopes of finding them sometime in the future on their peninsula.

These ships would become European artifacts and used accordingly. In 1928 A.D., the Italian government knew when and where these ships were buried. They had at least 1,300 years of eyewitness reports because the behemoths could be seen under water if the sunlight hit the lake the right way. The waters of Lake Nemi were only 60 feet in depth in the place where the ships were sunk. Finally, there was a way to get at the ships and reveal their true magnitude to the world. Mussolini drained this lake with a feat of modern marvels to reveal these two ships to his Italian people. They built a museum around the two ships so they could conduct their study. This was done to make the connection between ancient and modern Rome so the people would feel wonderful about themselves and superior to others, to give them self-confidence, self- assurance, self-reliance, self-awareness, self-respect and pride, to prepare them mentally for war, a war they almost won.

At the end of WWII, the Russian Army forced the Nazi's to retreat. The Russians were hot on their tails. The Nazi's retreated back to Lake Nemi and set the ships on fire in hopes that it would distract the Russian Army long enough for them to escape. It worked. When the Russians got there and saw those ancient day behemoths on fire they stopped in their tracks, dropped their guns and tried in vain to put the fire out, all the while forgetting about their enemy. Unfortunately, only a few pieces of these ships survive today. It turns out that some European ship builders and architects are going to design and build both ships from scratch from the detailed drawings the Italian government sketched after having possession of these behemoths for 15 years.

What is most exciting however, is the fact that whatever technique the Europeans use to rebuild these two ocean liners today, is the same technique the Africans used to build them more than 5,000 years ago in Alexandria, Egypt. Imagine inner city children knowing this fact about their ancestors. What would it do to them? More than likely the knowledge of these megaships and their true origin would evoke the same response in the African as it did in the European, it would eventually unify them and start a revolution.

Back in Alexandria, these huge behemoths arrived and departed the African harbor at least 200 times daily, twice as many making port at New York harbor today. Where do you take a ship 250 feet long, on average powered by wind and steam? Steam produced by water heated by battery generated electric power this time. The slot cars are now used to go through a conductor (toaster wires) to heat the containers that hold the water to make the steam push the ship plus to produce artificial light. This steam is also used to pressurize the plumbing system so you can have hot and cold running water, heating and air conditioning, showers and flushing toilets.

These conductors will produce heat for as long as the batteries are alive. There could have been a supply of batteries on board. The batteries could have been recharged with the steam just like our car batteries today are recharged by gasoline. If there is no wind to fill the cannabis sails to push the ship in the proper heading then the steam power could be used either in concert or as back up to the wind for continuity.

These huge pleasure palaces were navigated with the use of a complex computing machine known today as the Antikythera Mechanism. This mechanism was used to keep track of the sun, moon, planets and stars so that the crew and passengers of these luxury ocean liners and cargo ships would always know the time of day, the date of the year and their location on the earth. This should not seem far-fetched to you if you understand the significance of the zodiacs origin and the use of stars for navigation. Archeologists claim that the Antikythera Mechanism is of Greek origin and could not have come from anywhere else.

How could this be when the Greeks claimed that the earth is flat and the sun revolves around it? Today scientists and astronomers need a complex computer program to carry out exactly the function of this ancient mechanism. Again, where do you take a ship like this? You take a ship like this all over the world.

The Europeans claim that the Panama Canal is a modern feat of engineering. If we think about this critically, this can't be true. The world is talking about widening the canal today. Their ships are now too big to pass through it. Imagine their ships could not pass through the African Canal because it had not been maintained for more than 2,000 years.

Know this, when the European arrived in Central America, he was asking the natives about a waterway through the land. I wonder what inspired him to want to ask in the first place especially since he supposedly knew nothing about the Pacific Ocean or its existence at that time.

By the time the European thought about cutting through Panama to connect the Pacific and Atlantic Oceans, the first cut the Africans made was in ruins and reclaimed by the jungle. Today, the Europeans' Panama Canal must be maintained daily or the jungle will reclaim it. This is a constant battle.

The Africans did have business in the South American world before and during the Roman occupation. Africans needed the coca leaf and the tobacco leaf also. These products only grow in the Americas and the Africans purchased them from the indigenous people of South America. The Africans did not purchase them the same way the world does today and they did not use these products for the same reasons we use them today.

The African used the coca leaf and the tobacco leaf to purify and preserve their honored dead in the mummification process. They paid for these products with lady knowledge, using her to help the indigenous people build their cities in the clouds to watch over the harvest along the spine of the Andes Mountains. A German scientist found a 90% concentration of cocaine and tobacco levels in the body of an Egyptian mummy. This concentration level is impossible to live through, so these products were used strictly for the mummification process. The Germans tried to silence this female scientist to keep this information away from the masses, but to no avail.

Her research was presented on the Discovery Channel in the 1990's and has never been on television since. Again, cocaine and tobacco only grow in the Americas. No wonder the Europeans did not want this information to be found out, it implies too much. Truth is the Europeans and Arabs have been consuming the Africans honored dead for medicinal purposes for 830 years. In short, they have been getting high off the African mummies since 1150 A.D.

Opium, where anesthesia comes from, only grows in South East Asia. The Opium Flower was used in medical surgeries, like the caesarian section, made famous by Cleopatra and her baby's father Julius Caesar. Imagine cutting a baby out of a woman's womb without anesthesia, would the mother and child survive? Or would the female rather die knowing that both could die during the surgery?

Remember, Cleopatra took her family to Rome including Caesarean, the child the surgery is named after, to see his father while her African scientists struggled to fix the Roman calendar. Moreover, opium is the flower that Alexander the Great was to bring back to Africa as proof he made it to Asia and through the Persian army. How did the Africans know the opium flower was there in Asia in the first place? Africans used these products for the mummification process and for medical purposes respectively and respectfully.

These products of cocaine, tobacco and opium were carried back to Africa on these luxury ships as cargo. These cruises on 250 to 400-foot- long luxury ocean liners were also a part of the African mating ritual. Think about it, cruising around the world enjoying themselves in private suites, baths and libraries, basking in their own self-awareness, self- assurance, self-reliance, self-confidence, self-respect, and pride, passing the time teaching their children how to organize the stars. Today it is very difficult to tell what the African mating rituals are.

It should be noted that the origin of the Olmec civilization in Central America has been proved to be the Nubians from the Nile Valley. The Nubians spread their civilization throughout North and South America.

Nubia is over 26,000 years old, beginning with the Kingdom of Ta- Seti. Nubia is the mother of Egypt and if the Nubians traveled to the New World then so did the Egyptians. The countless common African artifacts found in the New World are a testament to this fact. There are also 100-ton Olmec busts carved out of solid granite found all over Central America that are shockingly Nubian in appearance. Remember, Colonel Piri Reis map, the oldest surviving map to show the Americas, was copied from a larger collection of world maps stolen from the Library of Alexandria. Do I have to declare the Africans had to discover the world first then survey it to create the collection of the world maps?

Nevertheless, the Nubians traveled north down the Nile River into the Mediterranean Sea, west through the straights of Gibraltar into the Atlantic Ocean around the west coast of Africa into the Gulf Stream west to Central America. In essence, they followed the wind gusts and ocean currents.

I am not sure of all of the details but it has come to my attention that something else took place in 1928 A.D. that justifies the African presence in the Americas. Something which was very exciting and unprecedented. Angered by the inhumane treatment of Negroes in America, the Noble Drew

Ali, born in Chicago of the Amexem-Moor-Empire attended the 5th Pan American conference for indigenous nations. It was at this conference that the Moors were declared the oldest people on the planet and the indigenous people of North America, South America, and Central America. This land the Moors called the Amexem-Moor-Empire long before it was called the Americas.

As I understand it, these people of color did not take their grievances to the Pan American conference as blacks, African Americans or Negroes because these titles are not nationalities. White is not a nationality either, but Italian and German is. So, there is a difference. To stake their rightful claim to the land, they had to come up with a nationality. They came as Moors from the Washitaw Nation and presented the documents and treaties that proved their claim. Of course, Noble Drew Ali was assassinated for this action but not before he put things into motion- things that cannot be reversed. He successfully snatched all the land from Alaska to Argentina from under the Europeans nose.

In 1994 A.D, Noble Drew Ali's great-great-grand daughter took the same grievance to the United Nations and won Australia and New Zealand as well. The UN voted on the Moors claim and 143 countries agreed with the claim while 4 opposed it or rejected the claim. Not surprisingly, these countries are the United States, Canada, Australia and New Zealand. These four countries reject the claim of the Moors because Europeans control these countries. After the UN decision, the Europeans are now considered invaders, foreigners, and aliens with no rights to the land at all. The documents are in Geneva Switzerland, "The World Court" waiting for the Moors to rise up out of their mental coma and claim the land as a people. This is truly a mighty blow to the European power structure and demands more research.

This claim/decision implies that the African was already here and established in America long before slavery. Moreover, this also implies that the kidnapping of Africans, transporting to the Americas and transforming them into slaves was not as robust and immense as we've been led to believe. Think about it, the Europeans attempted to bring 172,000,000 Africans over to the New World. 22,000,000 survived and 150,000,000 did not; they died on their way over. Now, 172,000,000 divided by 800 Africans per ship is 215,000 ship loads of Africans. Now, divide the 215,000 by the number of years the transportation of Africans took place, which is 423 years. So, 215,000 divided by 423 is 508.27 trips per year. Then you must divide 508.27 by the length of time each voyage took, which is 3 months. There are four 3-month periods in a year. Therefore, it works out to be 127.1 trips the Europeans took every three months, nonstop.

You must understand the European did all this work nonstop for very little profit because over 87% of these Africans died on the way over. The mathematics screams improbability. Not to mention the cold weather 6 months out of the year in the North Atlantic from November to April. The hurricanes season from June to October that rampaged through the same region and the logistics of food, drinking water and supplies for crew and cargo to survive the voyage. Here's something to think about, when did they have time to build and maintain the ships?

The Europeans have admitted that this feat cannot be duplicated today even if they only transported 22,000,000 Africans and all survived. The claim/decision also explains where most, if not all of the free blacks, especially the educated free blacks came from that put this country together while slavery was in full swing. It also explains why it was so easy for the runaway slaves to bond, blend, and relate to the Native Americans/ Indians because in fact, they were of the same complexion. These black/Indian tribes include; The Washitaw, The Yanasee, The Iroquois, The Cherokee, The Blackfoot, The Pequot and The Mohican. We have been led to believe that the slave trade was the only vehicle to the new world for Africans. To prevent them from knowing their own ancestral technology which made them the true masters of the 7 seas plus to keep them from making rightful claims to the land. I think the ultimate questions are; How did the Moors lose control of this land? And, why did the Moors conduct business with the Europeans in the first place?

Let me reiterate, if you declare yourself Black, African American or Negro you are accepting a title given to you by your slave master. You are declaring, not knowing it, that you were their cargo with no rights to this land and as of 1871 A.D. a $14^{th}$ Amendment citizen or a citizen under their established nation with no previous nationality of your own. You have no power and no claim to the land as the indigenous people of the land under their titles. Remember, the European never asked you do you want to be a $14^{th}$ Amendment citizen. He declared you are a $14^{th}$ Amendment citizen without a choice. This information definitely deserves more research.

It should not be difficult to believe that the mega ships that made port in Alexandria 200 times a day were not limited to the Mediterranean Sea but actually circumnavigated the globe. In fact, logic dictates this given their size and shape. You must remember that Alexandria marks the beginning of the end of the highest civilization the world has ever known. It follows that the ancient maps of the world that are just as accurate as the maps of today did not come from extraterrestrials but from the great black man who mapped out the entire planet.

So, when you hear of the Barbarian Viking "Eric the Red" traveling to the Americas in his little row boat, know that the black man did it bigger, better and much earlier and did it in luxurious comfort and style.

## Noble Drew Ali
## The invisible man who changed things.

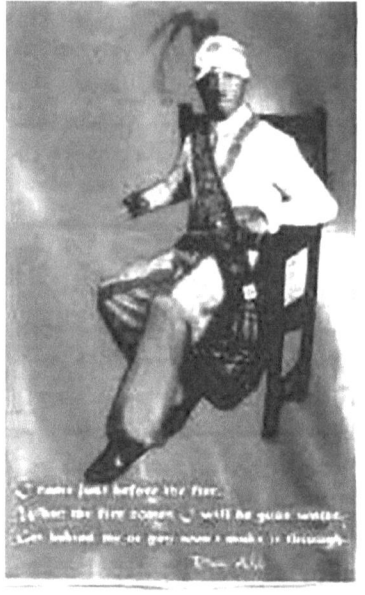

*Africa: It's True Role in the Ancient World* •

Note: the size of the ship compared to the humans standing around it.

# SECTION 17

# European Contribution to Society

Jeremiah (1: 14-16) "Then the Lord said unto me; Out of the North, an evil shall break forth upon all the inhabitants of the land." So, what is the European contribution to society anyway? I have learned that it is definitely not civilization; rather, it is the perfected use of slave labor, oppression, depression, suppression, exploitation, inquisitions, massive book burning campaigns, a police force, prisons, old-folks-homes and thanks to the philosopher, Nostradamus, the loaded handgun. Thank God Queen Cleopatra shut down the power plant so the romans would not have a working model. Thank God Alexander the Great did not make it all the way to Southeast Asia or gunpowder would have been under the Europeans control much earlier. Europeans discovered gunpowder during Marco Polo's lifetime, between 1254 A.D. and 1324 A.D. The first gun powdered powered cannon was produced during this period a full 4,400 years after Alexander's death according to Mer- enjuiti. Moreover, the European didn't get electricity until 1883 A.D., a full 62 years after deciphering our language; this is a full 1,917 years after Queen Cleopatra shut down the power plant. So, don't ever say that there isn't a God because if the Europeans found gunpowder earlier or had access to electricity back then, all of us, every brown body would be a beast of burden to this day.

God gave the African an out. His plan is greater than we could possibly imagine. So just think of yourselves as chess pieces and God is playing through you against the fallen angel. The fallen angel, whose name is Set (Seth), suggested that God take everything away from his chess pieces but their lives so Set could make a move. The demon couldn't even make a move until the Lord accommodated him. Just like the story of Job in the Bible. What power the Africans must have had. God understood all the demon wanted was his chess pieces, so he left himself a way out, covertly, with a chess move done under the demon's nose.

The Lord moved gunpowder to Southeast Asia and out of the demon's hands until it would be too late for a complete takeover. Doesn't this sound like a familiar account to you?

Don't you let him down. Get an education so you can see the Lords face again. Notice that black starts second in chess to give the other pieces their only chance of survival. We can speculate that the Europeans decided on this rule of chess after he was introduced to the game in the 1400's then killing the ones that made the original rules up during the Spanish Inquisition.

What are the characteristics of these other chess pieces anyway? These other chess pieces are parasites with a memory of the game and who really rules the board: taking pride in knowing that the Lord's pieces do not remember who they are anymore, due to their combined efforts, this is what gives them their focus, their edge. All we need is a unifying factor like our control over electricity and the bond we have with each other as the first in everything that makes life good plus the control and discipline to use it for the good of others no matter how immature they choose to be.

People will say that this book is based on speculation and unfounded evidence and therefore should not be seen as scholarly or factual. I say history (his-story) has been written by those who have hanged heroes, I say the European's version is a hoax trumped up to make him look superior, to make up for his inferiorities. Did you know that this version of lies is also considered scholarly and factual by the academic community and has been accepted as truth for over 2,000 years?

Moreover, the European is the academic community controlling what is learned. In truth, I have learned that Europe is really the dark territory making little to no positive contribution to mankind. It is everything that the African continent has been called over the years, over the centuries. It is time to decide for yourself what the truth really is. Ezekiel (39:5-7) And I will send a fire to Magog (Son of Japheth (Genesis (10:2))) and among them that dwell carelessly in the coast lands; And they shall know that I am the Lord.

# SECTION 18

# Today and Beyond

Rome has been held in high regard as the pinnacle of the ancient world for centuries. Even the designer of downtown Detroit was a lover of Rome. He studied Rome intently, reading everything he could on the city. He even changed his name from Elias Brevoort Woodward to Augustus Brevoort Woodward in honor of Rome's second ruler and the one to conquer Egypt, making Rome an empire, Caesar Augustus.

After the devastating fire of 1805 A.D., Detroit needed to be rebuilt because of its significance as an international port. Thomas Jefferson, now President of the United States, appointed his friend Augustus B. Woodward to rebuild the capital of the Michigan territories. Woodward designed downtown Detroit's infrastructure. He drew up a system of hexagonal street blocks with Grand Circus Park at its center. Ironically, his infrastructure plan for Detroit is derived literally from the infrastructure of Rome, which he studied. What is most interesting is that Rome's infrastructure is derived literally from the Egyptian Kingdom of Alexandria, which has its infrastructure derived literally from the Egyptian Kingdoms of Memphis, Heliopolis, and Luxor/Karnak where Alexander the Great went to see what a Kingdom should look like and how it should be designed and built.

Detroit is truly an African city of African design. When you are looking at downtown Detroit, you are really looking at a revival of downtown Alexandria. After Augustus B. Woodward's death, the main avenue separating the east side of Detroit from the west side was renamed after him in honor of his memory.

Believe it or not, the scenario I have described in this book concerning the relationship between the African and the European is so deep within the recesses of our minds that there are three mega-billion- dollar blockbuster movie epics that have the very essence of this scenario as their story line or theme. The first is Star Wars, number 1-6. This movie is about the force of good being betrayed by the force of evil (the dark side). Everyone knows that the dark side used to be a part of the force of good. The dark side had ambitions, taking over everything by exterminating the good side to almost extinction with the help of an army of clone machines. Later a savior comes and reestablishes the kingdom and this time an indefinite one.

The second is the Terminator, numbers 1-3. This movie is about the humans building machines to help man. The machines become aware and later turn against its builders. The machines exterminate man almost to extinction despite rebellions. The humans finally win. Last but certainly not least we have the Matrix, numbers 1-3. This movie has a new element that is closer to the truth of what the Europeans did to the Africans, and is still being done today, that the other movies neglected. Let's see, the humans again build machines to help man. The machines become aware and later turn on the humans. The humans rebel. Then the machines capture the humans and turn them into batteries (Slaves).

Most interesting, the machines create a pseudo-reality for the batteries to live in to prevent future rebellions. This is done so the machines can thrive uncontested by the humans. (I wonder why machines have been made to be the enemy of man when in my experience they have helped me tremendously. I love my dishwasher, washing machine, clothes dryer, stove, refrigerator etc., as I am sure you do to. What is the subliminal message here?)

These movies and their uncanny accuracy to the African/European conflict are undeniable if you know the truth about the past. Hopefully you can see that the European knows the truth and is living off the fact that you don't. The question is what is the pseudo-reality created for the Africans in the real world that mimic the pseudo-reality in the Matrix trilogy?

It is religion. Christianity, along with all other theistic belief systems, is the fraud of the age. **It serves to detach the human species from the natural world and likewise, each other.** It supports blind submission to authority. It reduces human responsibility to the effect that God controls everything and in turn dreadful crimes can be justified in the name of a divine pursuit. Most importantly, it empowers those who know the truth but use the myth to manipulate and control societies. The religious myth is the most powerful device ever created and serves as the psychological soil upon which other myths can flourish. Think about it, the three major religious systems of this world are brand new, Christianity began between 325 A.D. and 400 A.D., Islam began in 671 A.D. and Judaism began in 500 A.D. The African was the original Christian, the original Muslim as well as the original Jew and was always religious. He is the catalyst of all three of these religious systems that have all been corrupted by others with a hidden agenda. These three systems all give credit to each other for their concepts but none will give credit to the African. Today, you cannot question any one of the three and the proponents of which will not accept the truth about these religious systems even when it is staring them in the face.

Many people have struggled to bring the African story to light. This is the African legacy; a legacy that saw the mastery of every natural and supernatural discipline conceived. This legacy is the creator of western civilization, all religious systems and the modern world, period. Africans had a mastery of knowledge and understanding in applied mathematics and science that lead to the zenith of civilization in the Nile Delta. Mathematics is the language through which the Almighty designed the Universe, a universe described with science.

This is why these subjects are so important and so powerful. Mathematics, contrary to popular belief, is a language that was not created by man. It was discovered and the African was the first to master this language and through it, discovered God. The evidence is overwhelming, so without a working knowledge of these subjects, one can find our story unbelievable, and since the African story is unbelievable it was easy for the European to claim it. But only after the Romans killed the people with the knowledge and then burned the knowledge base, did Europeans claim the remaining stolen knowledge for themselves and then distorted history for the sake of confusion.

The African has been oppressed for 2,100 years and has still risen to the top of his field in all areas of study. African people have invented and discovered thousands of new products and mechanisms to help mankind despite the fact that the Africans are depicted as tree monkeys from a backwards continent. Africans have been mis-educated for a reason. I have discovered that reason through the powers of mathematics, physical science, biology, chemistry, operations research, probability theory, statistics and a desire to know more about the African contribution. I was not taught it in school but I knew Africans had to have done something good in this world despite what I had been told by the mainstream.

I have used these disciplines to analyze the evidence, even the obvious fact that these disciplines are the evidence themselves for the simple fact that they are on paper. Paper that use to be a tree, let alone blank. I have discovered the truth and the truth hurts. If I can get to the inner-city elementary school student through the elementary school teacher and instill the math in them properly to provide an excellent base, then the elementary school student will one day come to these same conclusions that I have.

Over time there will be a rise in math proficiency. I will free more Africans this way so they can join me in my pain so that we can together end this insanity by ignoring the oppressor and impose our own list of proposals, i.e. demands on the European; and finally move forward as a nation again establishing our fathers unending kingdom. Hosea (13:4) Yet, I am the Lord, thy God, from the land of Egypt and thou shalt know no God but me; for there is no Savior besides me. So, it is written. So, let it be done… again.

Downtown Detroit's Skyline.
(In the image of Alexandria, Egypt)

## The 7-8 Wonders of the Ancient World

| Name | Where | European Dates | African Dates | Status |
|---|---|---|---|---|
| Sphinx | Egypt | 2500 B.C. | 17,500 B.C. | Present |
| Pyramid Complex | Egypt | 2500 B.C. | 10,500 B.C. | Present |
| Hanging Gardens | Babylon Pre-Persia | 600 B.C.-400 A.D. | ?3350 B.C.- 400 A.D. | Reclaimed by the desert |
| Temple of Artemis | Persia West Turkey | 560 B.C. - 356 B.C. | ?3270 B.C. - ?3160 B.C. | Lightning burns it down |
| Temple of Artemis Rebuilt | Persia West Turkey | 280 B.C. - 480 A.D. | ?3080 B.C. - 480 A.D. | Destroyed by Attila the Hun |
| Tomb of Mausolus | Persia West Turkey | 353 B.C. - 700 A.D. | ?3130 B.C. - 700 A.D. | Destroyed by an earthquake |
| Lighthouse of Alexandria | Egypt | 250 B.C. - 1480 A.D. | 3111 B.C. - 1480 A.D. | Destroyed by an earthquake |
| Statue of Zeus Amon-Ra | Greece | 433 B.C. - 391 A.D. | 433 B.C. - 391 A.D. | Dismantled by Theodosius I |
| Colossus of Rhodes | Greece | 280 B.C. - 224 B.C. | 280 B.C. - 224 B.C. | Destroyed by an earthquake |

Here is a short list of a few people who went to Africa and departed with something that made them better...

| God | Religion | Philosophy | Conquerors |
|---|---|---|---|
| Jesus | Abraham | Socrates | Alexander the Great |
|  | Joseph | Plato | Julius Caesar |
|  | Jacob | Aristotle | Napoleon |
|  | Muhammad |  | The Arabs |
|  | Isaac |  | Cyrus the Great |

| Medicine | Mechanics | Mathematics | Architecture |
|---|---|---|---|
| Galen | Heron | Euclid | Solomon |
| Hypocrites | Archimedes | Pythagoras |  |

# Time Lines

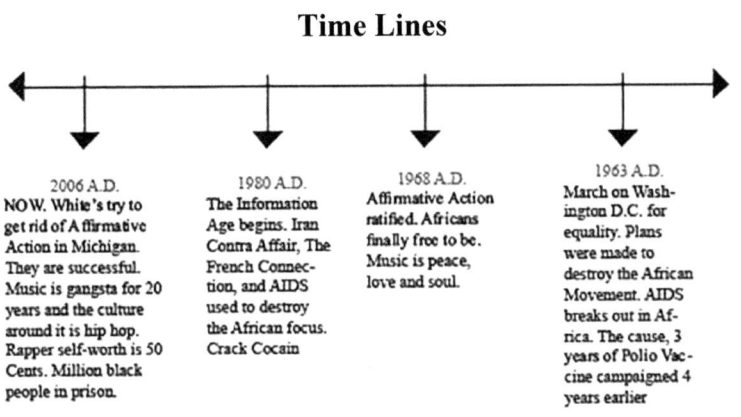

**2006 A.D.**
NOW. White's try to get rid of Affirmative Action in Michigan. They are successful. Music is gangsta for 20 years and the culture around it is hip hop. Rapper self-worth is 50 Cents. Million black people in prison.

**1980 A.D.**
The Information Age begins. Iran Contra Affair, The French Connection, and AIDS used to destroy the African focus. Crack Cocain

**1968 A.D.**
Affirmative Action ratified. Africans finally free to be. Music is peace, love and soul.

**1963 A.D.**
March on Washington D.C. for equality. Plans were made to destroy the African Movement. AIDS breaks out in Africa. The cause, 3 years of Polio Vaccine campaigned 4 years earlier

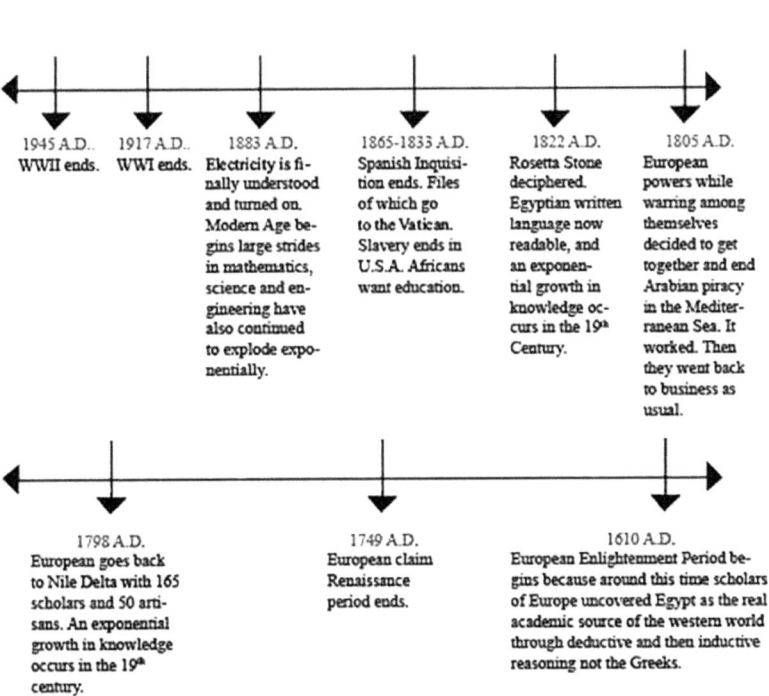

**1945 A.D.**
WWII ends.

**1917 A.D.**
WWI ends.

**1883 A.D.**
Electricity is finally understood and turned on. Modern Age begins large strides in mathematics, science and engineering have also continued to explode exponentially.

**1865-1833 A.D.**
Spanish Inquisition ends. Files of which go to the Vatican. Slavery ends in U.S.A. Africans want education.

**1822 A.D.**
Rosetta Stone deciphered. Egyptian written language now readable, and an exponential growth in knowledge occurs in the 19th Century.

**1805 A.D.**
European powers while warring among themselves decided to get together and end Arabian piracy in the Mediterranean Sea. It worked. Then they went back to business as usual.

**1798 A.D.**
European goes back to Nile Delta with 165 scholars and 50 artisans. An exponential growth in knowledge occurs in the 19th century.

**1749 A.D.**
European claim Renaissance period ends.

**1610 A.D.**
European Enlightenment Period begins because around this time scholars of Europe uncovered Egypt as the real academic source of the western world through deductive and then inductive reasoning not the Greeks.

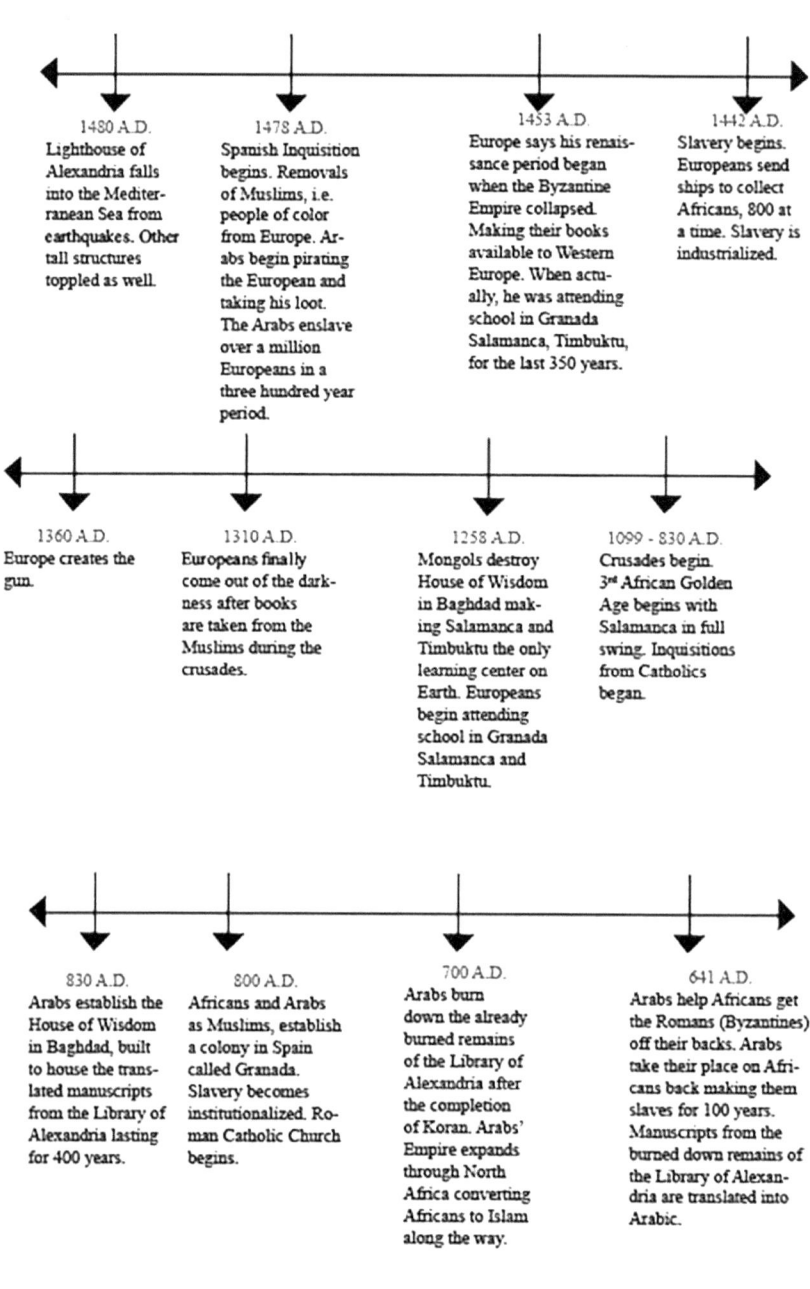

*Africa: It's True Role in the Ancient World* •

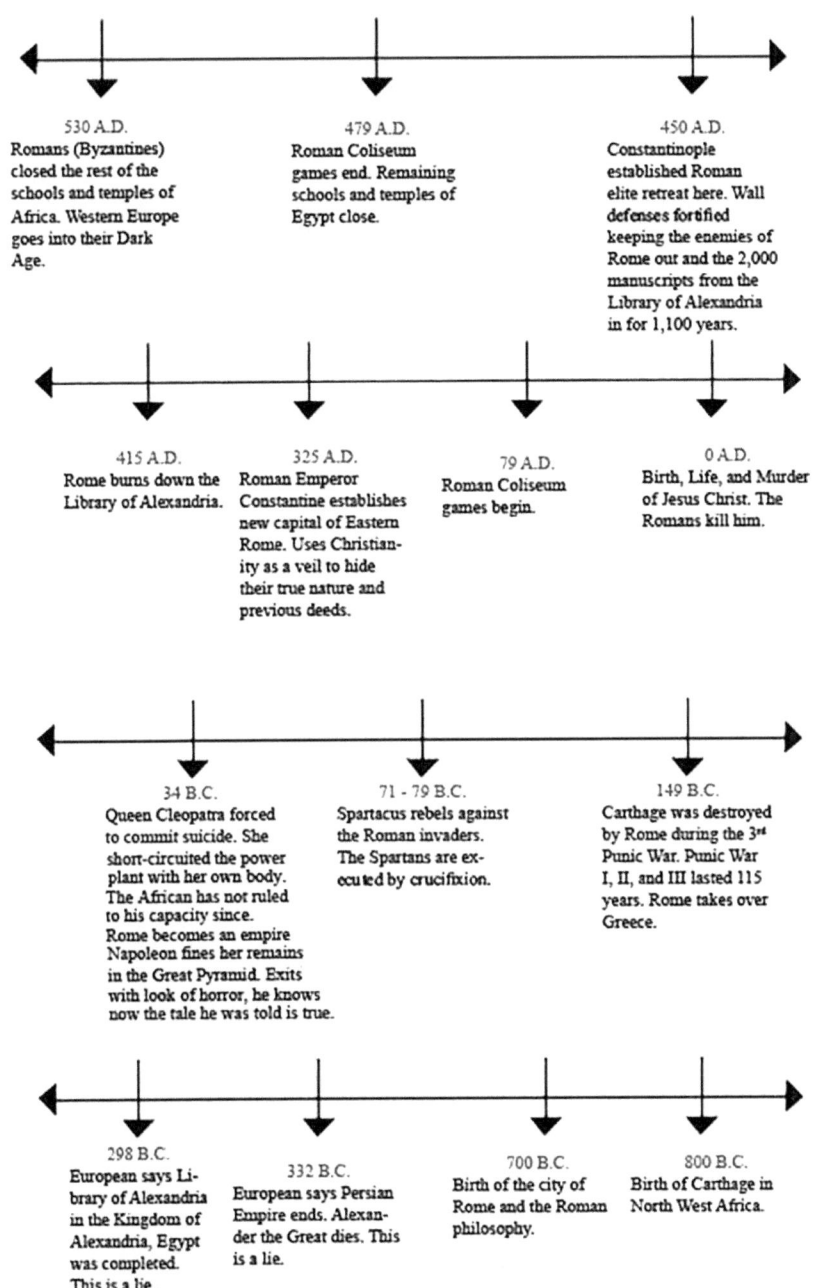

530 A.D.
Romans (Byzantines) closed the rest of the schools and temples of Africa. Western Europe goes into their Dark Age.

479 A.D.
Roman Coliseum games end. Remaining schools and temples of Egypt close.

450 A.D.
Constantinople established Roman elite retreat here. Wall defenses fortified keeping the enemies of Rome out and the 2,000 manuscripts from the Library of Alexandria in for 1,100 years.

415 A.D.
Rome burns down the Library of Alexandria.

325 A.D.
Roman Emperor Constantine establishes new capital of Eastern Rome. Uses Christianity as a veil to hide their true nature and previous deeds.

79 A.D.
Roman Coliseum games begin.

0 A.D.
Birth, Life, and Murder of Jesus Christ. The Romans kill him.

34 B.C.
Queen Cleopatra forced to commit suicide. She short-circuited the power plant with her own body. The African has not ruled to his capacity since. Rome becomes an empire Napoleon fines her remains in the Great Pyramid. Exits with look of horror, he knows now the tale he was told is true.

71 - 79 B.C.
Spartacus rebels against the Roman invaders. The Spartans are executed by crucifixion.

149 B.C.
Carthage was destroyed by Rome during the 3rd Punic War. Punic War I, II, and III lasted 115 years. Rome takes over Greece.

298 B.C.
European says Library of Alexandria in the Kingdom of Alexandria, Egypt was completed. This is a lie.

332 B.C.
European says Persian Empire ends. Alexander the Great dies. This is a lie.

700 B.C.
Birth of the city of Rome and the Roman philosophy.

800 B.C.
Birth of Carthage in North West Africa.

• *Matthew Theodore Momon*

1200 B.C.
European says Greece begins but as a learning center, not a nation.

2000 B.C.
European says Persian Empire begins, this is a lie.

3111 B.C.
Professor Mer-enjiuti says Greece and Africa were married. Says Alexander's Kingdom and University begins. Europeans massively educated. A 2nd African Golden Age starts. The pure African rule over Egypt ends with the 30th Dynasty mating with the family of Ptolemy I, the 2nd European Pharaoh of Egypt. 6th Wonder of the World, the Lighthouse turned on.

3200 B.C.
Alexander the Great 1st European Pharaoh dies. Rids the Mediterranean World of the Persians. Greece becomes a nation.

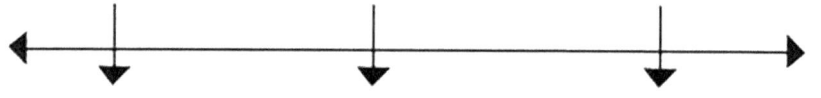

3294 - 3500 B.C.
Birth of Macedonia later called Greece. 22nd Dynasty, Libyans (Tamahu aka white people) attack Egypt and take over. Nubians save Egypt and expel the Tamahu, reestablishing black rule during the 25th Dynasty. Persian Army invades both the south and north sides of the Mediterranean Sea during 27th Dynasty. Greek city/states constantly fighting each other.

4000 B.C.
Egyptians teach Socrates. The creation of European thought begins 6,000 years before present, being educated for the first time for free.

4000 - 4525 B.C.
Hyksos (whites from the North) enslave Africa for 265 years, expelled by Ahmose I of the 18th Dynasty. Hittites (whites from the North) disrupted Africa for 260 years, expelled by Ramesses II of the 19th Dynasty. Egypt expands its boarders consuming Jordan, Syria, and Iraq into Upper Euphrates River. These blacks would later be known as the Cannanites who were later expelled by the northern Jews from Caucus Mountains. In 70 A.D. these were also the black people of Masada who chose mass suicide instead of Roman humiliation.

*Africa: It's True Role in the Ancient World* •

**5006 B.C.**
During the 7th dynastic period, Europeans (Troglodytes) came into Lybia from the north and attacked Egypt from the west. They were later expelled by Mentuhotep II, of the 11th Dynasty, 43 years later who then unifies Egypt again.

**6000 B.C.**
Radar and sonar confirm the age of the Sahara desert. Sand completely covered this region pushing civilization up against the current position of the Nile.

**6015 B.C.**
Persian Empire begins with Nomadic Tribes.

**6025 B.C.**
Followers of Set fight followers of his brother Osiris and lose and are expelled to the north of Africa again. King Menes, Narmer, (Scorpion King) establishes the 1st of the 30 human dynasties says Professor Mer-enjiuti. The first Golden Age after the Ice Age begins.

**6000 - 10,025 B.C.**
Then followed a dynasty of 30 Demigods who reigned for 3,650 years. Then for 350 years there was no rule over Egypt. Ice Age ends.

**10,500 B.C.**
Divine rulers, deities (Gods) finish Pyramid Complex. Belt of Orion's Star system could be superimposed perfectly on top of the Pyramid Complex, marking their birth. The desert begins its relentless approach to the Niles new and current position.

**11,500 B.P.**
Beginning of the end of the Ice Age due to polar shift. Nile changes direction. Extinction of Woolly Mammoth, Saber Tooth Tiger, and their foods. Atlantis disappears under Antarctic ice.

**17,500 B.P.**
Africans fashioned the largest freestanding statue in the world; the Sphinx with Heru's head on it to honor him after he banished Set's army to the frozen wasteland beyond the Mediterranean Sea.

**18,000 B.P.**
War of the Gods and men. Set kills his brother Osiris (Orion). The wife of Osiris, Isis, gave birth to Heru. Heru killed his uncle Set and reestablished his father's kingdom then banished Set's army north of Africa.

Peace on Earth, good will towards man.

Earth is Heaven and man is God

# ABOUT THE AUTHOR

I was born in 1968 A.D. I shared the womb with my twin brother, Christopher Floyd Momon. My brother was a healthy baby; I wasn't, I was born two pounds, three ounces. My mother told me that the doctors were ready to conclude the operation when they noticed me. After entering the world, the doctor performed their normal routine on me but I did not respond to their attempts to wake me. They put me in an incubator to simulate the womb then told my parents that I had a 50% chance of survival and if by some miracle I survived, I would be unable to see. This was all because of the cigarettes my parents smoked in the sixties. Back then it was considered cool, acceptable and healthy, even the doctors endorsed it. Today, we know better. The effects of smoking did not affect my brother and sister because they were of normal weight. I wasn't; so, it affected me most of all.

In my case, the doctors were incorrect. I survived but I spent the first 13 years of my life in and out of hospitals for eye surgeries. I spent the first years of my schooling in special education for the visually impaired. I also had asthma that I finally out grew with exercise. Psychologists will tell you that the first 12 years of an individual's life is known as "The Formative Years" and new parents will agree. This means that the essence of you is developed in those years. They are correct in many ways. For instance, I was not that sociable when I was young because I was in special education or involved in some way with eye surgery, so I find it difficult to be sociable today.

When my brother was outside playing, I was reading science and encyclopedia books when I could see well enough to read. I studied math because I was impressed with how far the planets are from each other, how far the stars were from each other and so on. After I received my Master's degree in Operation Research/Statistics from Michigan State University I wanted to follow up on what I asked my father when I was 10 years old. Back then my father and I were watching "The Ten Commandments" for the 5th time or so in my life while my father was drinking coffee and smoking a cigarette. As I recall, we were the only ones watching that show that day when I asked my father, "Dad, what did black people do?" and my father chuckled a little as if he knew something but could not tell me because he knew I would not have understood anything at that time.

After I graduated college I attended church for at least a year to see if that institution would teach me about the past but they would not because they have a closed view of the world. I was very disappointed in this institution so I bought some books from African bookstores like the Shrine of the Black Madonna. These books told me that the knowledge and the three major religious systems come from Africa plus they explained the history of the Nile Valley and the Mediterranean World. It was very moving; however, they did not track the path of the knowledge from Africa to the modern world. I had to wait 10 years (and I wasn't really waiting) until the movie Alexander the Great came out in 2006 A.D.

It was the catalyst for a broadcasting revolution. The movie Alexander the Great was so poorly done, so none historic that the History Channel put on a 2-hour documentary that was very well done and very informative. So much so that the other educational channels decided to follow suit. Channels like the Discovery Channel, A&E, TLC and PBS battled each other to put this history on T.V. From this battle I have acquired 36 hours of video documented evidence, but it was not enough. These channels were still following conservative views. To counter this view, I ordered 14 hours of video documented evidence from African scholars to fill the gaps.

I had to write about what I learned for two reasons, to organize the history for myself and to clear my mind. It was therapy for me and I hope it is for you as well.

# SPECIAL THANKS

To Mathematics and Science for allowing me to see the world from without. My mother and father, Carol M. Momon and Theodore S. Momon Jr., the griot sayers, Ashra and Merira Kwesi, Kemet Nu Productions, the archaeocryptographer Mr. Karl P. Munck, the honorable Dr. John Henrik Clarke, the focused laser Mrs. Sally Yee, the hunters of knowledge, Dr. Yosef Ben Jochannan, Dr. Ishakamus Barashango, Dr. Cheikha Anta Diop, Dr. Ivan Van Sertima, Dr. Hannibal Lavine Jr., Mr. Anthony Browder and Dr. Asa G. Hilliard III. Also, thanks to Mr. Myron Wimbush for setting up my publishing connection and printing.

If you have a comment or an opinion about this book and you want to express it I can be reached at the e mail address *momonmatt@gmail. com*

Next:

## **The Cosmology of the African:**
His ambition, inspiration and motivation to
understand everything about where he lives:

By
Matthew Theodore Momon

Printed by Libri Plureos GmbH in Hamburg, Germany